ROBERT BURNS
Poems selected by DON PATERSON

ROBERT BURNS

Poems selected by

DON PATERSON

faber and faber

This selection first published in 2001
by Faber and Faber Limited
3 Queen Square London WC1N 3AU

Photoset by Parker Typesetting Service, Leicester
Printed in Italy

A CIP record for this book
is available from the British Library
ISBN 0–571–20740–5

10 9 8 7 6 5 4 3 2 1

Contents

Introduction

Since the character of Robert Burns is so complicated as effectively not to exist at all – there is barely a human trait which he did not exhibit at one time or another, as if it somehow *defined* him – everyone is free to make their own reading of Burns according to their own personal, critical or neurotic agenda. The net result of such uninhibited speculation is that Burns's complexity is now a more straightforward business than the endless and contradictory simplifications to which he has been subjected. In some ways 'complex' doesn't do him justice: the more closely any aspect of Burns's life or work is scrutinised, the less coherent the picture becomes. No doubt this kind of fractal disintegration is as true of any life as of any coastline, but Burns, whose interior war-cry appears to have been *grit your teeth and think of the biographers*, seems to have done everything in his power to compound it.

I think it's a doomed project to attempt to reconstruct Burns's character from his correspondence, as so many have done; its volume is no guarantee of its reliability. All it confirms is Burns's furious shapeshifting, and there is no reason to believe he inhabited one character with any less sincerity than another, even though one Robert Burns might later comment wryly on another's conduct. Burns had a genius for fastening on the form of address best able to manipulate the emotions and affections of each correspondent, through a brilliant mix of insight, impersonation and flattery, both concealed and unconcealed. His lift stopped at every floor from service to penthouse, and he would emerge conversing fluently in the tongue with which his interlocutor felt most comfortable. This was far more than mere sleekitness: it was achieved by his having organised his language, through a prodigious feat of intellect, into a continuum which ran without interruption from low Ayrshire Scots to high Johnsonian English. Burns's desire to be all things to all men, then, furnished him with the most remarkable linguistic resource any Scottish poet has ever had at their disposal, and his tragedy is, in part, the extent to which that resource was squandered.

The inability of the natural performer to manage a natural response leads to disaster when he makes the uncharacteristic mistake of being spontaneous. In Burns's letters and conversation, for every triumph of eloquence and manipulation (and triumphs they were: of invective, wheedling, satire, silver-tongued seduction, hard-nosed business talk, prostration and abasement, self-editorship and man-to-man bawdry) there is always one hideous miscalculation, with Burns telling his correspondent either far more than they needed to know, or quite the last thing they wanted to hear.

As a poet, conversely, Burns was at his best when most spontaneous. To consider something for too long generally gave him time to change his first and truest response; the world might embrace a fluent liar and dissembler, but the muse has little time for anything but the most transparent negotiations. As eloquent as he was in English, it was never Burns's native tongue; he had to think first, and this was generally fatal to the results. All his best work was written in Scots.

Most of the myths surrounding Burns are in a permanent state of recrudescence, and have to be dispatched annually. Burns was no 'heaven-taught ploughman', but an intellectually brilliant and deeply-read individual who could hold his own in the most sophisticated company. As usual, the error is partly Burns's own fault. He was cheerfully (and at the time, perhaps judiciously) complicit in the advertisement of his noble savagery: the preface to the Kilmarnock Edition is, amongst a thousand other things, a deservedly notorious exercise in false humility. Burns didn't fish for compliments; he went after them with an elephant gun.

Another myth concerns the business of Burns's universal popularity. Burns's Scots is a fairly exclusive register; even

Scots readers will struggle, in places, without a glossary. The supposed mystery of Burns's genius is this: if Burns's flower was entirely the product of his peculiar linguistic micro-climate, what made it so supernaturally robust that it could take root in so many other nations and tongues? The answer is that, much of the time, it didn't. What has been too often admired – by Scots and non-Scots alike – is not his poetry but his sloganeering: 'A Man's a Man', not 'The Second Epistle to J. Lapraik'. But this is still only half the story, and there remains a deeper truth to Burns's broad appeal.

Much of it comes down, I think, to Burns's most important insight, which is that the spiritual, the social, the sexual, the natural and the political are coterminous and even consubstantial human realms – not competing sensitiv-ities that happen to be sharing the same organism. Burns felt that if you sang one, you should sing them all. The contradictions they present are only apparent – or if real, then at least as necessary and integral a part of the human dream as any other. For me, Burns teaches that if we keep those realms continually in dialogue, each tempers, modifies and refines the laws of the others; the traffic increases between the boundaries they do share, while those they do not are drawn the more firmly. From this process a crucial moral distinction emerges: hypocritical behaviour becomes far less forgivable, merely inconsistent behaviour far more so. Burns destroys Holy Willie for his hypocrisy, not his inconsistency. Burns's truest song is very simple, and it goes: *Man is complicated*. This insight was assisted by the fact that Burns himself was about as inconsistent an individual as it is possible to be and still remain sane.

The 'Address to the Unco Guid' is Burns's most explicit exposition of this stance. Superficially the poem might seem a hymn to moral relativity, and certainly at one level it is no more than a retrospective defence of Burns's almost comic inability to keep it in his breeks. Burns, though, is not the first poet to find his greatest and fieriest eloquence in self-justification; the poem soon transcends its dubious occasion with the argument that the self-aware soul can act, in the end, only according to an inscrutable interior *mores* – one shaped by the unique patterns of pressure, attraction and resistance that constitute the weather of the individual mind.

It's also one of the few occasions where Burns successfully uses his full range. The poem's almost imperceptible stanza-by-stanza modulation from Scots to High English – I can't help but be reminded of some of the canons in Bach's *Musical Offering* – is a small miracle of rhetoric. ('A Vision' and 'To a Mountain-Daisy' attempt the same thing, but with a far less comfortable gradient.) The terrific sophistication of the last stanza also demonstrates what Burns had it in his grasp to achieve had he taken Donne or Shakespeare and not Gray and Shenstone as his exemplars.

As is often the case with autodidacts, Burns was helplessly susceptible to influence. It was, on the whole, a bad age in which to carry this trait. His English verse was destroyed, in part, by the example of the aforementioned poets (not forgetting such contemporary bibles as *Letters Moral and Entertaining* by Mrs Elizabeth Rowe); mercifully, Allan Ramsay and Robert Fergusson had a marvellous effect on his Scots. Fergusson, brilliantly talented, hopelessly unstable, and radiating an intellectual confidence that the Scots tongue had not seen since the Makars, had died both recently and young enough to allow Burns to indulge a deep identification: their relationship was a straightforwardly mystical case of literary ventriloquism. It was a debt Burns often acknowledged, and Burns himself paid for a new stone to be erected over Fergusson's grave in the Canongate cemetery in Edinburgh. (This totem for his ghost-brother was commissioned from – at this point, we hear Jung chuckling in heaven – one Robert Burn.)

As I've mentioned, Burns was born in a lean time for verse. He was unfortunate not to have been born twenty years later, when, with far more stimulating company and better drugs, he would have made a fine Romantic. On the other hand, another fifty years on and he would have made a depressingly successful Victorian, so perhaps we should be grateful for what poetry he did manage to draw from the true spring before – and at how short a distance downstream – it was poisoned with the effluent of Augustan sentiment.

Sentimentalism is the art of professing to feel. *What* you profess to feel, and whether you do or do not feel it, is secondary to the business of making a hymn to your own sensitivity. Practically all Burns's poetry in English is thoroughly sentimental. If 'English Burns' were a violinist, we would now find him an intolerably syrupy performer, with a wide sob of a vibrato and not a phrase in his repertoire that we could not immediately identify from another source. But in an insecure, mediocre or disenfranchised age, familiarity always substitutes for epiphany, so it was little wonder that he took the Edinburgh salons by storm in the 1780s – or that, fatally, so many encouraged him to persist with his modest talents at the expense of his great gifts.

Burns may have been a second-rate violinist, but he was an incomparable fiddler. With the discipline gained from his classical training, Burns returned to the 'rustic lyre' as a virtuoso the likes of which the instrument had never seen. (This calls to mind Duke Ellington's remark that you need the street *and* the conservatoire.) Burns's subscription to Augustan ideals of linguistic comportment – while disastrous for his English verse – endowed his Scots with intellectual ambition, discipline of syntax, and a deep awareness of poetic artifice – as well as doubling his vocabulary at a stroke. Thrillingly, Burns stood at the linguistic crossroads where Milton meets Dunbar. This doubling of vocabulary is an important point: Burns's Scots, contrary to popular belief, is anything but pure – it's a sinewy, mongrel tongue always ready to import an English synonym, whether to raise the rhetorical stakes, or just to accommodate local exigencies of metre and rhyme.

When he chose to write in Scots, Burns was not so much lowering the tone as levelling it, so that the lord's dog could talk to the ploughman's – but also so that ideas had to stand on their own intrinsic merit, rather than rely on the cultural privilege of the language in which they happen to be couched. It's to be regretted that Burns never took this tactic anything like far enough, and that he lost faith in the poem just when he should have been pressing on to the next peak.

The root problem was that Burns was at heart a love-poet, and that his satirical, polemical and philosophical excursions were only possible while that principal conduit remained open. The dereliction of Burns's muse is no less strange and fascinating than that of Coleridge's or Rimbaud's: after the age of twenty-seven, he wrote very little poetry of any merit. The one exception is 'Tam o'Shanter', that marvellously febrile semi-cautionary tale, and possibly the easiest poem to psychoanalyse ever written (*vagina dentata* having apparently accounted for more than just the end of Maggie's tail: to my ear at least, the poem finishes about twelve lines too early). Thereafter, his energies were devoted largely to song-making.

Some have seen Burns's shift from poetry to song – song-writing, collecting, 'improving' – as a betrayal of his gift; Robert Louis Stevenson famously disparaged it as 'whittling cherry-stones'. I'd suggest, however, that we might think of it as a psychologically strategic transfer of allegiance from Erato to Euterpe, the former having failed him once too often. The promise of Erato is that the song will win love – and her ploy, to be true to the letter but not the spirit of that promise. The male poet can be kept productive by transferring the aura of the beloved elsewhere, as soon as the actual woman is won. If ever a man would have benefited from reading Robert Graves it was Burns.

There was always a kind of shifting tetragrammaton written on Burns's heart which, when interrogated, would spell out the name of the nearest available woman. After which it was only a matter of time before his own selfhood worked its contamination and the word was scrambled again (all the sooner if the unfortunate woman bought his entirely sincere declarations of love, and made the mistake of consummating the affair – the exact synonym of 'consummated', in Burns's psyche, being 'finished'). This is the uncertainty principle of love, where the value of the beloved is destabilised by the unreliable beholder. In Burns, as I've mentioned before, you can see whatever you want to see; with that qualification in mind, I still cannot help reading into his feverish concupiscence a terrible self-hatred. He tried to assuage it by proving that every woman loved him, but any course of action motivated by such a feeling can only end in its tragic reaffirmation. As A. L. Kennedy has pointed out, Burns, the man who more than anything else adored the company of women, would ultimately learn that his presence in a room was enough to blacken a woman's name.

That hardwired internal connexion between love and poetry had probably been overloaded for some time, but one woman shorted it out for good: the brilliant, beautiful, and almost superstitiously chaste Nancy McLehose. Although Burns seemed resigned to his fickle muse (a fact into which we can read raging egotism and neurosis, but not misogyny; Burns was forever guiltily picking up the tab for his amorous catastrophes), he still knew the dream-woman when he saw her. Their infamous epistolary exploits as 'Sylvander and Clarinda' have embarrassed and amused generations, but to dismiss these merely as neoclassical camp is to do a disservice to a couple who were clearly deeply in love, and trying to bridge an impossible social gap. Even for Burns, it stands out as a particularly desperate and moving performance, driven equally by an adolescent desire to impress, an intolerable sexual frustration and a deep and genuine emotion. It got him, in the end, nowhere. To have expended every ounce of his eloquence and come away empty-handed was a betrayal too far. In such circumstances a man has to curse someone, and as a natural self-hater Burns had to look no further than his shaving mirror.

By then Burns knew two things: that he was never going to find his intellectual equal in a woman of his own class, and that elsewhere his low pedigree would forever count against him. He might be lionised in the clubs and an honoured guest at the dining-table, but elsewhere the caste-system was as strongly enforced as ever. Burns was never quite Edinburgh's dancing bear, but it was only a matter of time before a man of such high and low self-regard would start to feel like one.

Burns's enthusiasm for the great song-collecting project had been earlier fired on a long tour of Scotland, made during a bout of post-Edinburgh tristesse. (His Scottish peregrinations may also have been an unconscious and slightly pathetic impersonation of the Grand Tour he was unable to afford.) His allegiance to poetry – whatever his conscious mind was telling him – was probably already shaken. Poems, unlike songs, tend to have an ulterior motive; otherwise they would just say what they mean and be done with it. After Nancy, however, there was no secret freight, there now being nothing to be smuggled over the border, nothing to be breached, nothing to be won. Burns's skills as love-poet, his artful duplicities, were suddenly redundant. All that was left to him, if he was to go on singing at all, was to sing for its own sake.

There was a positive aspect to this: Burns found a way of assuaging his terminally fragmented personality by project-ing it into a vast and partly anonymous work. It was, in a way, a natural move; from being all things to all men, it's a fairly short step to being no one at all. Burns's revitalisation of Scottish song was so pervasive that its extent can never be fully known. It is a Song of Songs, an abstract and mythic lovemaking where Burns's muse – as prefigured in 'A Vision' – now wears the dress of nationhood. Back home in Ayrshire, Burns set up his lyric dockyard, and spent his last ten years fitting out an old and dilapidated fleet with fine new sails. The work was so skilfully executed that, two hundred years later, it is still going strong.

At this point, I suppose I should own up to an absolute horror of poems set to music. A setting of a good poem is, for me, the sound of something working out the terms of its own redundancy. Poems are already set to music. Musical 'enhancement' can only undermine or exaggerate an effect, so that the result is either discord or melodrama. Too often Burns is wheeled out as the supposed clincher against this argument: but Burns's lyrics are not poems. Hearing them sung, we are indubitably in the presence of poetry, but as an illusion created by the magical stereoscopic collusion of the two arts. The printed lyric remains imbued with the echo of the song, and it's this that allows us to elevate it, mistakenly, to the status of poetry. Knowing that I'm as prone to this sentimental delusion as the next person, I have included only a handful of the lyrics here. This is not to diminish the importance of that part of Burns's enterprise, but a recognition of the fact that it can't be adequately represented in this medium. No one who has heard, say, Dick Gaughan sing 'Westlin' Winds' ('Song Composed in August') can pretend that the version which appears on the page is the true form, any more than the sheet-music is the melody.

One reason why it is rare for a good poet to make a good lyricist is that song-writing consists in the ruthless cancellation of so many of the effects poets prize most highly. The lyricist's strategy (not that it can't be varied, of course, particularly in the comic song) is to say what you mean while making as little extraneous noise as possible, so that nothing detracts from the melody. Most poets find this an infuriating stricture, and either refuse to recognise it - always with dreadful results – or sensibly avoid writing lyrics altogether. Burns's peerless status as a lyricist reflects a remarkable ability to subdue his expressive gift to the service of the song.

Many of the other poems included here are in the six-line verse-form of the Standard Habbie. This consists of three lines of four stresses, one of two, one of four, then another of two, and is rhymed AAABAB. Its name derives from Robert Sempill of Beltrees' elegy to the piper Habbie Simpson, though the stanza is far older, and has its origins, predictably, in the repertoire of the Provençal troubadours. The Habbie was to Burns what *terza rima* was to Dante or the ballad to Emily Dickinson: it was perfectly fitted to the turn of his thought, and in return (here we allude to one of poetry's occult sciences) it also came to educate the pattern which his thought subsequently took.

One of the reasons the Habbie has fallen into near-disuse is that, with its mixture of tricksy rhymes and long pauses on the dimeter lines, it positively encourages the accommodation of both humorous and grave registers within the same poem: this sits beautifully with Burns's project of showing the whole man. In our less emotionally sophisticated times, it sometimes seems as if those registers have been assigned to entirely different genres. Shorter lines also tend to have the effect of concretising language. A longer line usually gave Burns too much time, so that language curdles into abstraction, which in his case meant sentiment, opinion, or – least attractively – judgement. The Habbie operated as a natural safeguard against that tendency. It is also an exercise in controlled excess, in how far you can go too far: with its six lines, but only two rhymes, the effort can easily start to show – though in the right hands this strain can be turned to brilliant comic effect. (The Habbie therefore carries a far more self-conscious sense of its own artifice than other verse-forms, and is a grand stanza for the natural show-off or smart Alec: enter our man.) These rhymes are often feminine, in part because Scots possesses a wealth of trochaic words and diminutives, diminutives being symptoms of the national diseases of litotes and overfamiliarity.

Elsewhere Burns offsets this, typically, by proving himself a master of overstatement too. While this was something he mercifully reserved for his Augustan verse (though we can see some of its tiresome theatricality even in fine poems like 'To a Mountain-Daisy'), in another life it might have served him as a useful operatic register. Ted Hughes was amongst those afflicted by the same condition, against which the standard objection must be raised that it takes no longer – and no more imaginative expenditure – to type the word 'sausage' or 'trousers' than 'death' or 'universe'. Hughes's work, though, is redeemed by its complete lack of sentimentality. Burns had no such luck. In the fruity exorbitancies of his English verse the flow of sense is always from species to genus, which, unless you have something like Pope's flair for tell-not-show, is usually death to the poem. But in the best of his Scots poems, Burns gave the universal a specific life, the only kind it can ever have.

It's a feature of genius that it often completes the journeys before it has actually travelled the course. This impatience can lead to boredom and burn-out, to short-cuts and premature codas. For whatever reason, Burns was not the poet he should have been; but measuring how far he fell short of his own promise is no excuse for ignoring his real accomplishments. Burns's current low critical stock amongst many English readers (the 200th anniversary of his death in 1997 was met with an almost swaggering indifference from the Southron literati) is due as much to the Scots' own catastrophic mismanagement of Burns's estate as to unexamined racism. The greatest service the Scots could perform would be to rescue Burns from his own bardolatry, and there have been recent signs (not the least of which is an important volume of critical essays edited by Robert Crawford, *Robert Burns and Cultural Authority*) that Burns's genie has at least begun to negotiate his parole, albeit still from within his sealed shortie tin.

Though in bleaker moments, you sometimes feel that not until the last Supper has been eaten, and the Judas kiss of his last biographer planted, will Burns be free of himself. Robert Burns died of being Robert Burns, as RLS remarked, and has continued dying of him ever since. It's to be hoped that Scotland's growing political autonomy will play a part in this. Nations in abeyance have a far greater need for the fripperies of nationhood than do active ones, and perhaps one day we will see the ludicrous post of 'national bard', along with the *Flower of Scotland*, the Gathering of the Clans and the Edinburgh Tattoo all go down the same plughole.

Then, perhaps, Burns will be accorded his true place in the literary constellation. Burns was such a flash act that his after-image still blinds the page; the Scots can barely see to read their other poets. His rehabilitation, then, is also dependent on the rehabilitation of those – from Montgomerie to Fergusson to Soutar – who have been unfairly eclipsed by his radiance. But even when the charts have been redrawn and each poet shines by no more nor less than their own light, you suspect there will be one star, variable, iridescent and riven, still burning more fiercely than all the others.

Don Paterson

ROBERT BURNS

Song, composed in August

I

Now westlin winds, and slaught'ring guns
    Bring Autumn's pleasant weather;
The moorcock springs, on whirring wings,
    Amang the blooming heather:
Now waving grain, wide o'er the plain,
    Delights the weary Farmer;
The moon shines bright, as I rove at night,
    To muse upon my Charmer.

II

The Pairtrick lo'es the fruitfu' fells;
    The Plover lo'es the mountains;
The Woodcock haunts the lanely dells;
    The soaring Hern the fountains:
Thro' lofty groves, the Cushat roves,
    The path o' man to shun it;
The hazel bush o'erhangs the Thrush,
    The spreading thorn the Linnet.

III

Thus ev'ry kind their pleasure find,
    The savage and the tender;
Some social join, and leagues combine;
    Some solitary wander:
Avaunt, away! the cruel sway,
    Tyrannic man's dominion;
The Sportsman's joy, the murd'ring cry,
    The flutt'ring, gory pinion!

IV

But PEGGY dear, the ev'ning 's clear,
    Thick flies the skimming Swallow;
The sky is blue, the fields in view,
    All fading-green and yellow:
Come let us stray our gladsome way,
    And view the charms o' Nature;
The rustling corn, the fruited thorn,
    And ilka happy creature.

V

We'll gently walk, and sweetly talk,
    While the silent moon shines clearly;
I'll clasp thy waist, and fondly prest,
    Swear how I lo'e thee dearly:
Not vernal show'rs to budding flow'rs,
    Not Autumn to the Farmer,
So dear can be, as thou to me,
    My fair, my lovely Charmer!

Pairtrick, *partridge*; Cushat, *wood pigeon*; ilka, *every*

Poor Mailie's Elegy

Lament in rhyme, lament in prose,
Wi' saut tears trickling down your nose;
Our *Bardie*'s fate is at a close,
   Past a' remead!
The last, sad cape-stane of his woes;
   Poor Mailie's dead!

It 's no the loss o' warl's gear,
That could sae bitter draw the tear,
Or make our *Bardie*, dowie, wear
   The mourning weed:
He 's lost a friend and neebor dear,
   In *Mailie* dead.

Thro' a' the town she trotted by him;
A lang half-mile she could descry him;
Wi' kindly bleat, when she did spy him,
   She ran wi' speed:
A friend mair faithfu' ne'er came nigh him,
   Than *Mailie* dead.

I wat she was a *sheep* o' sense,
An' could behave hersel wi' mense:
I'll say 't, she never brak a fence,
   Thro' thievish greed.
Our *Bardie*, lanely, keeps the spence
   Sin' *Mailie*'s dead.

Or, if he wanders up the howe,
Her living image in *her yowe*,
Comes bleating to him, owre the knowe,
   For bits o' bread;
An' down the briny pearls rowe
   For *Mailie* dead.

She was nae get o' moorlan tips,
Wi' tauted ket, an' hairy hips;
For her forbears were brought in ships,
        Frae 'yont the TWEED:
A bonier *fleesh* ne'er cross'd the clips
        Than *Mailie* 's dead.

Wae worth that man wha first did shape,
That vile, wanchancie thing – *a raep*!
It maks guid fellows girn an' gape,
        Wi' chokin dread;
An' *Robin*'s bonnet wave wi' crape
        For *Mailie* dead.

 O, a' ye *Bards* on bonie DOON!
An' wha on AIRE your chanters tune!
Come, join the melancholious croon
        O' *Robin*'s reed!
His heart will never get aboon!
        His *Mailie* 's dead!

cape-stane, *keystone*; dowie, *melancholy*; mense, *decorum*; spence,
parlour; howe, *dale*; yowe, *ewe*; knowe, *hillock*; tips, *rams*; tauted ket,
matted fleece; clips, *shears*; wanchancie, *unlucky*; raep, *rope*; aboon, *above*,
up

6

Mary Morison

O Mary, at thy window be,
   It is the wish'd, the trysted hour;
Those smiles and glances let me see,
   That make the miser's treasure poor:
How blythely wad I bide the stoure,
A weary slave frae sun to sun;
   Could I the rich reward secure,
The lovely Mary Morison!

Yestreen when to the trembling string
   The dance gaed through the lighted ha',
To thee my fancy took its wing,
   I sat, but neither heard, nor saw:
Though this was fair, and that was braw,
   And yon the toast of a' the town,
I sigh'd, and said amang them a',
   'Ye are na Mary Morison.'

O Mary, canst thou wreck his peace,
   Wha for thy sake wad gladly die!
Or canst thou break that heart of his,
   Whase only faute is loving thee!
If love for love thou wilt na gie,
   At least be pity to me shown;
A thought ungentle canna be
   The thought o' Mary Morison.

stoure, *storm*; braw, *fine, handsome*

Address to the Unco Guid, or the Rigidly Righteous

> *My Son, these maxims make a rule,*
> *And lump them ay thegither;*
> *The* Rigid Righteous *is a fool,*
> *The* Rigid Wise *anither:*
> *The cleanest corn that e'er was dight*
> *May hae some pyles o' caff in;*
> *So ne'er a fellow-creature slight*
> *For random fits o' daffin*
>
> Solomon. (Eccles. 7: 16)

I

O ye wha are sae guid yoursel,
    Sae pious and sae holy,
Ye've nought to do but mark and tell
    Your Neebours' fauts and folly!
Whase life is like a weel-gaun mill,
    Supply'd wi' store o' water,
The heaped happer 's ebbing still,
    And still the clap plays clatter.

II

Hear me, ye venerable Core,
    As counsel for poor mortals,
That frequent pass douce Wisdom's door
    For glaikit Folly's portals;
I, for their thoughtless, careless sakes
    Would here propone defences,
Their donsie tricks, their black mistakes,
    Their failings and mischances.

III

Ye see your state wi' theirs compar'd,
    And shudder at the niffer,
But cast a moment's fair regard
    What maks the mighty differ;
Discount what scant occasion gave,
    That purity ye pride in,
And (what 's aft mair than a' the lave)
    Your better art o' hiding.

IV

Think, when your castigated pulse
    Gies now and then a wallop,
What ragings must his veins convulse,
    That still eternal gallop:
Wi' wind and tide fair i' your tail,
    Right on ye scud your sea-way;
But, in the teeth o' baith to sail,
    It maks an unco leeway.

V

See Social-life and Glee sit down,
    All joyous and unthinking,
Till, quite transmugrify'd, they're grown
    Debauchery and Drinking:
O would they stay to calculate
    Th' eternal consequences;
Or your more dreaded h—ll to state,
    D—mnation of expences!

VI

Ye high, exalted, virtuous Dames,
 Ty'd up in godly laces,
Before ye gie poor *Frailty* names,
 Suppose a change o' cases;
A dear-lov'd lad, convenience snug,
 A treacherous inclination –
But, let me whisper i' your lug,
 Ye're aiblins nae temptation.

VII

Then gently scan your brother Man,
 Still gentler sister Woman;
Tho' they may gang a kennin wrang,
 To step aside is human:
One point must still be greatly dark,
 The moving *Why* they do it;
And just as lamely can ye mark,
 How far perhaps they rue it.

VIII

Who made the heart, 'tis *He* alone
 Decidedly can try us,
He knows each chord its various tone,
 Each spring its various bias:
Then at the balance let 's be mute
 We never can adjust it;
What 's *done* we partly may compute,
 But know not what 's *resisted*.

unco guid, *very good*; dight, *winnowed*; daffin, *foolery*; core, *company*;
douce, *sober*; glaikit, *inattentive, foolish*; donsie, *hapless*; niffer,
comparison; lave, *rest*; aiblins, *perhaps*; kennin, *little*

Epistle to Davie, a Brother Poet

I

While winds frae off BEN-LOMOND blaw,
And bar the doors wi' driving snaw,
   And hing us owre the ingle,
I set me down, to pass the time,
And spin a verse or twa o' rhyme,
   In hamely, *westlin* jingle.
While frosty winds blaw in the drift,
   Ben to the chimla lug,
I grudge a wee the *Great-folk*'s gift,
    That live sae bien an' snug:
      I tent less, and want less
        Their roomy fire-side;
      But hanker, and canker,
        To see their cursed pride.

II

It 's hardly in a body's pow'r,
To keep, at times, frae being sour,
   To see how things are shar'd;
How *best o' chiels* are whyles in want,
While *Coofs* on countless thousands rant,
   And ken na how to wair 't:
But DAVIE lad, ne'er fash your head,
   Tho' we hae little gear,
We're fit to win our daily bread,
   As lang 's we're hale and fier:
      'Mair spier na, nor fear na,'
        Auld age ne'er mind a feg;
      The last o't, the warst o't,
        Is only but to beg.

III

To lye in kilns and barns at e'en,
When banes are craz'd, and bluid is thin,
   Is, doubtless, great distress!
Yet then *content* could make us blest;
Ev'n then, sometimes we'd snatch a taste
   Of truest happiness.
The honest heart that 's free frae a'
   Intended fraud or guile,
However Fortune kick the ba',
   Has ay some cause to smile:
      And mind still, you'll find still,
        A comfort this nae sma';
      Nae mair then, we'll care then,
        Nae *farther* we can *fa'*.

IV

What tho', like Commoners of air,
We wander out, we know not where,
   But either house or hal'?
Yet *Nature*'s charms, the hills and woods,
The sweeping vales, and foaming floods,
   Are free alike to all.
In days when Daisies deck the ground,
   And Blackbirds whistle clear,
With honest joy, our hearts will bound,
   To see the *coming* year:
      On braes when we please then,
        We'll sit and *sowth* a tune;
      Syne *rhyme* till 't, we'll time till 't,
        And sing 't when we hae done.

V

It 's no in titles nor in rank;
It 's no in wealth like *Lon'on Bank*,
    To purchase peace and rest;
It 's no in makin muckle, *mair*:
It 's no in books; it 's no in Lear,
    To make us truly blest:
If Happiness hae not her seat
    And center in the breast,
We may be *wise*, or *rich*, or *great*,
    But never can be *blest*:
        Nae treasures, nor pleasures
            Could make us happy lang;
        The *heart* ay 's the part ay,
            That makes us right or wrang.

VI

Think ye, that sic as *you* and *I*,
Wha drudge and drive thro' wet and dry,
    Wi' never-ceasing toil;
Think ye, are we less blest than they,
Wha scarcely tent us in their way,
    As hardly worth their while?
Alas! how aft, in haughty mood,
    GOD's creatures they oppress!
Or else, neglecting a' that 's guid,
    They riot in excess!
        Baith careless, and fearless,
            Of either Heaven or Hell;
        Esteeming, and deeming,
            It a' an idle tale!

Then lest us chearfu' acquiesce;
Nor make our scanty Pleasures less,
　　By pining at our state:
And, ev'n should Misfortunes come,
I, here wha sit, hae met wi' some,
　　An 's thankfu' for them yet.
They gie the wit of *Age to Youth*;
　　Then let us ken oursel;
They make us see the naked truth,
　　The *real* guid and ill.
　　　　Tho' losses, and crosses,
　　　　　　Be lessons right severe,
　　　　There 's *wit* there, ye'll get there,
　　　　　　Ye'll find nae other where.

VIII

But tent me, DAVIE, *Ace o' Hearts*!
(To say aught less wad wrang the *cartes*,
　　And flatt'ry I detest)
This life has joys for you and I;
And joys that riches ne'er could buy;
　　And joys the very best.
There 's a' the *Pleasures o' the Heart*,
　　The *Lover* and the *Frien'*;
Ye hae your MEG, your dearest part,
　　And I my darling JEAN!
　　　　It warms me, it charms me,
　　　　　　To mention but her *name*:
　　　　It heats me, it beets me,
　　　　　　And sets me a' on flame!

IX

O, all ye *Pow'rs* who rule above!
O Thou, whose very self art *love*!
 Thou know'st my words sincere!
The *life blood* streaming thro' my heart,
Or my more dear *Immortal part*,
 Is not more fondly dear!
When heart-corroding care and grief
 Deprive my soul of rest,
Her dear idea brings relief,
 And solace to my breast.
  Thou Being, Allseeing,
   O hear my fervent pray'r!
  Still take her, and make her,
   Thy most peculiar care!

X

All hail! ye tender feelings dear!
The smile of love, the friendly tear,
 The sympathetic glow!
Long since, this world's thorny ways
Had number'd out my weary days,
 Had it not been for you!
Fate still has blest me with a friend,
 In ev'ry care and ill;
And oft a more *endearing* band,
 A *tye* more tender still.
  It lightens, it brightens,
   The tenebrific scene,
  To meet with, and greet with,
   My Davie or my Jean!

O, how that *name* inspires my style!
The words come skelpan, rank and file,
   Amaist before I ken!
The ready measure rins as fine,
As *Phœbus* and the famous *Nine*
   Were glowran owre my pen.
My spavet *Pegasus* will limp,
   Till ance he 's fairly het;
And then he'll hilch, and stilt, and jimp,
    And rin an unco fit:
      But least then, the beast then,
       Should rue this hasty ride,
      I'll light now, and dight now,
       His sweaty, wizen'd hide.

ingle, *fireplace*; ben, *inside*; chiels, *lads*; Coofs, *fools, louts*; fier, *sound, healthy*; brae, *hillside*; Lear, *learning*; skelpan, *running*; spavet, *lame*; dight, *wipe, rub down*

Holy Willie's Prayer

And send the Godly in a pet to pray – Pope

Argument

Holy Willie was a rather oldish batchelor Elder in the parish of Mauchline, and much and justly famed for that polemical chattering which ends in tippling Orthodoxy, and for that Spiritualized Bawdry which refines to Liquorish Devotion. – In a Sessional process with a gentleman in Mauchline, a Mr Gavin Hamilton, Holy Willie, and his priest, father Auld, after full hearing in the Presbytry of Ayr, came off but second best; owing partly to the oratorical powers of Mr Robt Aiken, Mr Hamilton's Counsel; but chiefly to Mr Hamilton's being one of the most irreproachable and truly respectable characters in the country. – On losing his Process, the Muse overheard him at his devotions as follows –

O thou that in the heavens does dwell!
Wha, as it pleases best thysel,
Sends ane to heaven and ten to h–ll,
      A' for thy glory!
And no for ony gude or ill
      They've done before thee. –

I bless and praise thy matchless might,
When thousands thou has left in night,
That I am here before thy sight,
      For gifts and grace,
A burning and a shining light
      To a' this place. –

What was I, or my generation,
That I should get such exaltation?
I, wha deserv'd most just damnation,
      For broken laws
Sax thousand years ere my creation,
      Thro' Adam's cause!

When from my mother's womb I fell,
Thou might hae plunged me deep in hell,
To gnash my gooms, and weep, and wail,
      In burning lakes,
Where damned devils roar and yell
      Chain'd to their stakes. –

Yet I am here, a chosen sample,
To shew thy grace is great and ample:
I'm here, a pillar o' thy temple
      Strong as a rock,
A guide, a ruler and example
      To a' thy flock. –

[O L—d thou kens what zeal I bear,
When drinkers drink, and swearers swear,
And singin' there, and dancin' here,
      Wi' great an' sma';
For I am keepet by thy fear,
      Free frae them a'. –]

But yet – O L—d – confess I must –
At times I'm fash'd wi' fleshly lust;
And sometimes too, in warldly trust
      Vile Self gets in;
But thou remembers we are dust,
      Defil'd wi' sin. –

O L—d – yestreen – thou kens – wi' Meg –
Thy pardon I sincerely beg!
O may 't ne'er be a living plague,
      To my dishonor!
And I'll ne'er lift a lawless leg
      Again upon her. –

Besides, I farther maun avow,
Wi' Leezie's lass, three times – I trow –
But L—d, that friday I was fou
        When I cam near her;
Or else, thou kens, thy servant true
        Wad never steer her. –

Maybe thou lets this fleshy thorn
Buffet thy servant e'en and morn,
Lest he o'er proud and high should turn,
        That he 's sae gifted;
If sae, thy hand maun e'en be borne
        Untill thou lift it. –

L—d bless thy Chosen in this place,
For here thou has a chosen race:
But G—d, confound their stubborn face,
        And blast their name,
Wha bring thy rulers to disgrace
        And open shame. –

L—d mind Gaun Hamilton's deserts!
He drinks, and swears, and plays at cartes,
Yet has sae mony taking arts
        Wi' Great and Sma',
Frae G—d's ain priest the people's hearts
        He steals awa. –

And when we chasten'd him therefore,
Thou kens how he bred sic a splore,
And set the warld in a roar
        O' laughin at us:
Curse thou his basket and his store,
        Kail and potatoes. –

L—d hear my earnest cry and prayer
Against that Presbytry of Ayr!
Thy strong right hand, L—d, make it bare
          Upon their heads!
L—d visit them, and dinna spare,
          For their misdeeds!

O L—d my G—d, that glib-tongu'd Aiken!
My very heart and flesh are quaking
To think how I sat, sweating, shaking,
          And p—ss'd wi' dread,
While Auld wi' hingin lip gaed sneaking
          And hid his head!

L—d, in thy day o' vengeance try him!
L—d visit him that did employ him!
And pass not in thy mercy by them,
          Nor hear their prayer;
But for thy people's sake destroy them,
          And dinna spare!

But L—d, remember me and mine
Wi' mercies temporal and divine!
That I for grace and gear may shine,
          Excell'd by nane!
And a' the glory shall be thine!
          AMEN! AMEN!

splore, *riot, uproar*

Death and Doctor Hornbook
A True Story

Some books are lies frae end to end,
And some great lies were never penn'd:
Ev'n Ministers they hae been kenn'd,
      In holy rapture,
A rousing whid, at times, to vend,
      And nail 't wi' Scripture.

But this that I am gaun to tell,
Which lately on a night befel,
Is just as true 's the Deil 's in h–ll,
      Or Dublin city:
That e'er he nearer comes oursel
      'S a muckle pity.

The Clachan yill had made me canty,
I was na fou, but just had plenty;
I stacher'd whyles, but yet took tent ay
      To free the ditches;
An' hillocks, stanes, an' bushes kenn'd ay
      Frae ghaists an' witches.

The rising Moon began to glowr
The distant *Cumnock* hills out-owre;
To count her horns, wi' a' my pow'r,
      I set mysel,
But whether she had three or four,
      I cou'd na tell.

I was come round about the hill,
And todlin down on *Willie's mill*,
Setting my staff wi' a' my skill,
      To keep me sicker;
Tho' leeward whyles, against my will,
      I took a bicker.

I there wi' *Something* does forgather,
That pat me in an eerie swither;
An awfu' scythe, out-owre ae shouther,
        Clear-dangling, hang;
A three-tae'd leister on the ither
        Lay, large an' lang.

Its stature seem'd lang Scotch ells twa,
The queerest shape that e'er I saw,
For fient a wame it had ava,
        And then its shanks,
They were as thin, as sharp an' sma'
        As cheeks o' branks.

'Guid-een,' quo' I; 'Friend! hae ye been mawin,
'When ither folk are busy sawin?'
It seem'd to mak a kind o' stan',
        But naething spak;
At length, says I, 'Friend, whare ye gaun,
        'Will ye go back?'

It spak right howe – 'My name is *Death*,
'But be na' fley'd.' – Quoth I, 'Guid faith,
'Ye're maybe come to stap my breath;
        'But tent me, billie;
'I red ye weel, tak care o' skaith,
        'See, there 's a gully!'

'Gudeman,' quo' he, 'put up your whittle,
'I'm no design'd to try its mettle;
'But if I did, I wad be kittle
        'To be mislear'd,
'I wad na' mind it, no that spittle
        'Out-owre my beard.'

'Weel, weel!' says I, 'a bargain be 't;
'Come, gies your hand, an' sae we're gree't;
'We'll ease our shanks an' tak a seat,

        Come, gies your news!
'This while ye hae been mony a gate,
        'At mony a house.'

'Ay, ay!' quo' he, an' shook his head,
'It 's e'en a lang, lang time indeed
'Sin' I began to nick the thread,
        'An' choke the breath:
'Folk maun do something for their bread,
        'An' sae maun *Death*.

'Sax thousand years are near hand fled
'Sin' I was to the butching bred,
'And mony a scheme in vain 's been laid,
        'To stap or scar me;
'Till ane Hornbook 's ta'en up the trade,
        'And faith, he'll waur me.

'Ye ken *Jock Hornbook* i' the Clachan,
'Deil mak his king's-hood in a spleuchan!
'He's grown sae weel acquaint wi' *Buchan*,
        'And ither chaps,
'The weans haud out their fingers laughin,
        'And pouk my hips.

'See, here 's a scythe, and there 's a dart,
'They hae pierc'd mony a gallant heart;
'But Doctor *Hornbook*, wi' his art
        'And cursed skill,
'Has made them baith no worth a f—t,
        'D—n'd haet they'll kill!

''Twas but yestreen, nae farther gaen,
'I threw a noble throw at ane;
'Wi' less, I'm sure, I've hundreds slain;
        'But deil-ma-care!
'It just play'd dirl on the bane,
        'But did nae mair.

'*Hornbook* was by, wi' ready art,
'And had sae fortify'd the part,
'That when I looked to my dart,
          'It was sae blunt,
'Fient haet o't wad hae pierc'd the heart
          'Of a kail-runt.

'I drew my scythe in sic a fury,
'I nearhand cowpit wi' my hurry,
'But yet the bauld *Apothecary*
          'Withstood the shock;
'I might as well hae try'd a quarry
          'O' hard whin-rock.

'Ev'n them he canna get attended,
'Altho' their face he ne'er had kend it,
'Just sh— in a kail-blade and send it,
          'As soon 's he smells 't,
'Baith their disease, and what will mend it,
          'At once he tells 't.

'And then a' doctor's saws and whittles,
'Of a' dimensions, shapes, an' mettles,
'A' kinds o' boxes, mugs, an' bottles,
          'He's sure to hae;
'Their Latin names as fast he rattles
          'As A B C.

'Calces o' fossils, earths and trees;
'True Sal-marinum o' the seas;
'The Farina of beans and pease,
          'He has 't in plenty;
'Aqua-fontis, what you please,
          'He can content ye.

'Forbye some new, uncommon weapons,
'Urinus Spiritus of capons;
'Or Mite-horn shavings, filings, scrapings,

'Distill'd *per se*;
'Sal-alkali o' Midge-tail clippings,
        'And mony mae.'

'Waes me for *Johnny Ged's-Hole* now,'
Quoth I, 'if that thae news be true!
'His braw calf-ward whare gowans grew,
        'Sae white an' bonie,
'Nae doubt they'll rive it wi' the plew;
        'They'll ruin *Johnie*!'

The creature grain'd an eldritch laugh,
And says, 'Ye needna yoke the pleugh,
'Kirk-yards will soon be till'd eneugh,
        'Tak ye nae fear:
'They'll a' be trench'd wi' mony a sheugh,
        'In twa-three year.

'Whare I kill'd ane, a fair strae-death,
'By loss o' blood, or want o' breath,
'This night I'm free to tak my aith,
        'That *Hornbook*'s skill
'Has clad a score i' their last claith,
        'By drap and pill.

'An honest Wabster to his trade,
'Whase wife's twa nieves were scarce weel-bred,
'Gat tippence-worth to mend her head,
        'When it was sair;
'The wife slade cannie to her bed,
        'But ne'er spak mair.

'A country Laird had ta'en the batts,
'Or some curmurring in his guts,
'His only son for *Hornbook* sets,
        'And pays him well,
'The lad, for twa guid gimmer-pets,
        'Was Laird himsel.

'A bonie lass, ye kend her name,
'Some ill-brewn drink had hov'd her wame,
'She trusts hersel, to hide the shame,
'In *Hornbook*'s care;
'*Horn* sent her aff to her lang hame,
'To hide it there.

'That 's just a swatch o' *Hornbook*'s way,
'Thus goes he on from day to day,
'Thus does he poison, kill, an' slay,
An 's weel pay'd for 't;
'Yet stops me o' my lawfu' prey,
'Wi' his d–mn'd dirt!

'But hark! I'll tell you of a plot,
'Tho' dinna ye be speakin o't;
'I'll nail the self-conceited Sot,
'As dead 's a herrin:
'Niest time we meet, I'll wad a groat,
'He gets his fairin!'

But just as he began to tell,
The auld kirk-hammer strak the bell
Some wee, short hour ayont the *twal*,
Which rais'd us baith:
I took the way that pleas'd mysel,
And sae did *Death*.

Clachan, *the name of an ale-house*; yill, *ale*; canty, *merry*; stacher, *stagger*; tent, *heed, care*; leister, *pronged spear*; wame, *belly*; cheeks o' branks, *side-piece of a bridle*; billie, *friend*; skaith, *injury*; whittle, *knife*; kittle, *likely*; mislear'd, *mischievous*; king's-hood, *paunch*; spleuchan, *purse*; fient haet, *nothing, 'damn all'*; kail-runt, *stem of cabbage*; cowpit, *overturned*; kail-blade, *cabbage leaf*; calces, *powder*; Sal-marinum, *salt*; calf-ward, *churchyard* (fig.); gowans, *mayweed, dandelions*; sheugh, *ditch*; Wabster, *weaver*; batts, *colic*; twal, *twelve*

Epistle to J. Lapraik, An Old Scotch Bard

While briers an' woodbines budding green,
An' Paitricks scraichan loud at e'en,
And morning Poossie whiddan seen,
       Inspire my Muse,
This freedom, in an *unknown* frien',
       I pray excuse.

On Fasteneen we had a rockin,
To ca' the crack and weave our stockin;
And there was muckle fun and jokin,
       Ye need na doubt;
At length we had a hearty yokin,
       At *sang about*.

There was ae *sang*, amang the rest,
Aboon them a' it pleas'd me best,
That some kind husband had addrest,
       To some sweet wife:
It thirl'd the heart-strings thro' the breast,
       A' to the life.

I've scarce heard ought describ'd sae weel,
What gen'rous, manly bosoms feel;
Thought I, 'Can this be *Pope*, or *Steele*,
       Or *Beattie*'s wark;'
They tald me 'twas an odd kind chiel
       About *Muirkirk*.

It pat me fidgean-fain to hear 't,
An' sae about him there I spier't;
Then a' that kent him round declar'd,
       He had *ingine*,
That nane excell'd it, few cam near 't,
       It was sae fine.

That set him to a pint of ale,
An' either douse or merry tale,
Or rhymes an' sangs he'd made himsel,
        Or witty catches,
'Tween Inverness and Tiviotdale,
        He had few matches.

Then up I gat, an' swoor an aith,
Tho' I should pawn my pleugh an' graith,
Or die a cadger pownie's death,
        At some dyke-back,
A *pint* an' *gill* I'd gie them *baith*,
        To hear your crack.

But first an' foremost, I should tell,
Amaist as soon as I could spell,
I to the *crambo-jingle* fell,
        Tho' rude an' rough,
Yet crooning to a body's sel,
        Does weel eneugh.

I am nae *Poet*, in a sense,
But just a *Rhymer* like by chance,
An' hae to Learning nae pretence,
        Yet, what the matter?
Whene'er my Muse does on me glance,
        I jingle at her.

Your Critic-folk may cock their nose,
And say, 'How can you e'er propose,
'You wha ken hardly *verse* frae *prose*,
        'To mak a *sang*?'
But by your leaves, my learned foes,
        Ye're maybe wrang.

What 's a' jargon o' your Schools,
Your Latin names for horns an' stools;
If honest Nature made you *fools*,
        What sairs your Grammars?
Ye'd better taen up *spades* and *shools*,
        Or *knappin-hammers*.

A set o' dull, conceited Hashes,
Confuse their brains in *Colledge-classes*!
They *gang* in Stirks, and *come out* Asses,
        Plain truth to speak;
An' syne they think to climb Parnassus
        By dint o' Greek!

Gie me ae spark o' Nature's fire,
That 's a' the learning I desire;
Then tho' I drudge thro' dub an' mire
        At pleugh or cart,
My Muse, tho' hamely in attire,
        May touch the heart.

O for a spunk o' ALLAN's glee,
Or FERGUSON's, the bauld an' slee,
Or bright LAPRAIK's, my friend to be,
        If I can hit it!
That would be *lear* eneugh for me,
        If I could get it.

Now, Sir, if ye hae friends enow,
Tho' *real friends* I b'lieve are few,
Yet, if your catalogue be fow,
        I'se no insist;
But gif ye want ae friend that 's true,
        I'm on your list.

I winna blaw about *mysel*,
As ill I like my fauts to tell;
But friends an' folk that wish me well,
        They sometimes roose me;
Tho' I maun own, as monie still,
        As far abuse me.

There's ae *wee faut* they whiles lay to me,
I like the lasses – Gude forgie me!
For monie a Plack they wheedle frae me,
        At dance or fair:
Maybe some *ither thing* they gie me
        They weel can spare.

But MAUCHLINE Race or MAUCHLINE Fair,
I should be proud to meet you there;
We'se gie ae night's discharge to *care*,
        If we forgather,
An' hae a swap o' *rhymin-ware*,
        Wi' ane anither.

The *four-gill chap*, we'se gar him clatter,
An' kirs'n him wi' reekin water;
Syne we'll sit down an' tak our whitter,
        To chear our heart;
An,' faith, we'se be *acquainted* better
        Before we part.

Awa ye selfish, warly race,
Wha think that havins, sense an' grace
Ev'n love an' friendship should give place
        To *catch-the-plack*!
I dinna like to see your face,
        Nor hear your crack.

But ye whom social pleasure charms,
Whose hearts the *tide of kindness* warms,
Who hold your *being* on the terms,
     'Each aid the others,'
Come to my bowl, come to my arms,
     My friends, my brothers!

But to conclude my lang epistle,
As my auld pen 's worn to the grissle;
Twa lines frae you wad gar me fissle,
     Who am, most fervent,
While I can either sing, or whissle,
     Your friend and servant.

Poossie, *hare*; whiddon, *running*; Fasteneen, *Shrove Tuesday*; rockin,
spinning party; fidgean-fain, *excited*; ingine, *genius*; pleugh, *plough*;
graith, *gear*; crambo-jingle, *doggerel verse*; Stirk, *young bullock*; Plack,
coin; kirs'n, *christen*; whitter, *liquor*; gar me fissle, *get me excited*

To the Same
(*Second Epistle to J. Lapraik*)

WHILE new-ca'd kye rowte at the stake,
An' pownies reek in pleugh or braik,
This hour on e'enin's edge I take,
        To own I'm debtor,
To honest-hearted, auld LAPRAIK,
        For his kind *letter*.

Forjesket sair, with weary legs,
Rattlin the corn out-owre the rigs,
Or dealing thro' amang the naigs
        Their ten-hours bite,
My awkart Muse sair pleads and begs,
        I would na write.

The tapetless, ramfeezl'd hizzie,
She 's saft at best an' something lazy,
Quo' she, 'Ye ken we've been sae busy
        'This month an' mair,
'That trough, my head is grown right dizzie,
        'An' something sair.'

Her dowf excuses pat me mad;
'Conscience,' says I, 'ye thowless jad!
'I'll write, an' that a hearty blaud,
        'This vera night;
'So dinna ye affront your trade,
        'But rhyme it right.

'Shall bauld LAPRAIK, the *king o'hearts*,
'Tho' mankind were a *pack o' cartes*,
'Roose you sae weel for your deserts,
        'In terms sae friendly,
'Yet ye'll neglect to shaw your parts
        'An' thank him kindly?'

Sae I gat paper in a blink,
An' down gaed *stumpie* in the ink:
Quoth I, 'Before I sleep a wink,
     'I vow I'll close it;
'An' if ye winna mak it clink,
     'By Jove I'll prose it!'

Sae I've begun to scrawl, but whether
In rhyme, or prose, or baith thegither,
Or some hotch-potch that 's rightly neither,
     Let time mak proof;
But I shall scribble down some blether
     Just clean aff-loof.

My worthy friend, ne'er grudge an' carp,
Tho' Fortune use you hard an' sharp;
Come, kittle up your *moorlan harp*
     Wi' gleesome touch!
Ne'er mind how Fortune *waft* an' *warp*;
     She's but a b–tch.

She 's gien me monie a jirt an' fleg,
Sin' I could stridle owre a rig;
But by the L—d, tho' I should beg
     Wi' lyart pow,
I'll laugh, an' sing, an' shake my leg,
     As lang 's I dow!

Now comes the *sax an' twentieth* simmer,
I've seen the bud upo' the timmer,
Still persecuted by the limmer
     Frae year to year;
But yet, despite the kittle kimmer,
     I, Rob, am here.

Do ye envy the *city-gent*,
Behint a kist to lie an' sklent,
Or purse-proud, big wi' cent per cent,
      An' muckle wame,
In some bit *Brugh* to represent
      A *Baillie*'s name?

Or is 't the paughty, feudal *Thane*,
Wi' ruffl'd sark an' glancin cane,
Wha thinks himsel nae *sheep-shank bane*,
      But lordly stalks,
While caps an' bonnets aff are taen,
      As by he walks?

'O *Thou* wha gies us each guid gift!
'Gie me o' *wit* an' *sense* a lift,
'Then turn me, if *Thou* please, *adrift*,
      'Thro' Scotland wide;
'Wi' *cits* nor *lairds* I wadna shift,
      'In a' their pride!'

Were this the *charter* of our state,
'On pain o' *hell* be rich an' great,'
Damnation then would be our fate,
      Beyond remead;
But, thanks to *Heav'n*, that 's no the gate
      We learn our *creed*.

For thus the royal *Mandate* ran,
When first the human race began,
'The social, friendly, honest man,
      'Whate'er he be,
' 'Tis *he* fulfils *great Nature's plan*,
      'And none but *he*.'

O *Mandate*, glorious and divine!
The followers o' the ragged Nine,
Poor, thoughtless devils! yet may shine
      In glorious light,
While sordid sons o' Mammon's line
      Are dark as night!

Tho' here they scrape, an' squeeze, an' growl,
Their worthless nievefu' of a *soul*,
May in some *future carcase* howl,
      The forest's fright;
Or in some day-detesting *owl*
      May shun the light.

Then may LAPRAIK and BURNS arise,
To reach their native, kindred skies,
And *sing* their pleasures, hopes an' joys,
      In some mild sphere,
Still closer knit in friendship's ties
      Each passing year!

kye, *cattle*; rowte, *bellow*; forjesket, *exhausted*; tapetless, *foolish*;
ramfeezl'd, *fatigued*; dowf, *listless*; jirt, *jerk*; fleg, *kick*; lyart, *grey*; pow,
head; timmer, *timber*; limmer, *whore, mistress*; kittle, *fickle*; kimmer,
young girl; kist, *coffer*; paughty, *proud, haughty*; sark, *shirt*; nievefu',
handful

A Poet's Welcome to his love-begotten Daughter
The first instance that entitled him to the venerable
appellation of Father

Thou's welcome, Wean! Mischanter fa' me,
If thoughts o' thee, or yet thy Mamie,
Shall ever daunton me or awe me,
      My bonie lady;
Or if I blush when thou shalt ca' me;
      Tyta, or Daddie. –

Tho' now they ca' me, Fornicator,
And tease my name in kintra clatter,
The mair they talk, I'm kend the better;
      E'en let them clash!
An auld wife's tongue 's a feckless matter
      To gie ane fash. –

Welcome! My bonie, sweet, wee Dochter!
Tho' ye come here a wee unsought for;
And tho' your comin I hae fought for,
      Baith Kirk and Quier;
Yet by my faith, ye're no unwrought for,
      That I shall swear!

Wee image o' my bonie Betty,
As fatherly I kiss and daut thee,
As dear and near my heart I set thee,
      Wi' as gude will,
As a' the Priests had seen me get thee
      That 's out o' h—. –

Sweet fruit o' monie a merry dint,
My funny toil is no a' tint;
Tho' ye come to the warld asklent,
        Which fools may scoff at,
In my last plack your part 's be in 't,
        The better half o't. –

Tho' I should be the waur bestead,
Thou 's be as braw and bienly clad,
And thy young years as nicely bred
        Wi' education,
As any brat o' Wedlock's bed,
        In a' thy station. –

[Lord grant that thou may ay inherit
Thy Mither's looks an' gracefu' merit;
An' thy poor, worthless Daddie's spirit,
        Without his failins!
'Twad please me mair to see thee heir it
        Than stocked mailins!]

For if thou be, what I wad hae thee,
And tak the counsel I shall gie thee,
I'll never rue my trouble wi' thee,
        The cost nor shame o't,
But be a loving Father to thee,
        And brag the name o't.

Tyta, *pet name for father*; kintra, *country*; fash, *care*; Queir, *choir*; daut, *pet*; dint, *occasion*; tint, *lost*; asklent, *askew*; bestead, *placed*; bienly, *comfortably*; mailins, *holdings*

The Vision. Duan First

THE sun had clos'd the *winter-day*,
The Curlers quat their roaring play,
And hunger'd Maukin taen her way
      To kail-yards green,
While faithless snaws ilk step betray
      Whare she has been.

The Thresher's weary, *flingin-tree*,
The lee-lang day had tir'd me;
And when the Day had clos'd his e'e,
      Far i' the West,
Ben i' the *Spence*, right pensivelie,
      I gaed to rest.

There, lanely, by the ingle-cheek,
I sat and ey'd the spewing reek,
That fill'd, wi' hoast-provoking smeek,
      The auld, clay biggin;
And heard the restless rattons squeak
      About the riggin.

All in this mottie, misty clime,
I backward mus'd on wasted time,
How I had spent my *youthfu' prime*,
      An' done nae-thing,
But stringing blethers up in rhyme
      For fools to sing.

Had I to guid advice but harket,
I might, by this, hae led a market,
Or strutted in a Bank and clarket
      My *Cash-Account*;
While here, half-mad, half-fed, half-sarket,
      Is a' th' amount.

I started, mutt'ring blockhead! coof!
And heav'd on high my wauket loof,
To swear by a' yon starry roof,
          Or some rash aith,
That I, henceforth, would be *rhyme-proof*
          Till my last breath –

When click! the *string* the *snick* did draw;
And jee! the door gaed to the wa';
And by my ingle-lowe I saw,
          Now bleezan bright,
A tight, outlandish *Hizzie*, braw,
          Come full in sight.

Ye need na doubt, I held my whisht;
The infant aith, half-form'd, was crusht;
I glowr'd as eerie 's I'd been dusht,
          In some wild glen;
When sweet, like *modest Worth*, she blusht,
          And stepped ben.

Green, slender, leaf-clad *Holly-boughs*
Were twisted, gracefu', round her brows,
I took her for some SCOTTISH MUSE,
          By that same token;
And come to stop those reckless vows,
          Would soon been broken.

A 'hare-brain'd, sentimental trace'
Was strongly marked in her face;
A wildly-witty, rustic grace
          Shone full upon her;
Her *eye*, ev'n turn'd on empty space,
          Beam'd keen with *Honor*.

Down flow'd her robe, a *tartan* sheen,
Till half a leg was scrimply seen;
And such a *leg*! my bonie JEAN
          Could only peer it;
Sae straught, sae taper, tight and clean,
          Nane else came near it.

Her *Mantle* large, of greenish hue,
My gazing wonder chiefly drew;
Deep *lights* and *shades*, bold-mingling, threw
          A lustre grand;
And seem'd, to my astonish'd view,
          A *well-known* Land.

Here, rivers in the sea were lost;
There, mountains to the skies were tost:
Here, tumbling billows mark'd the coast,
          With surging foam;
There, distant shone, *Art*'s lofty boast,
          The lordly dome.

Here, DOON pour'd down his far-fetch'd floods;
There, well-fed IRWINE stately thuds:
Auld, hermit AIRE staw thro' his woods,
          On to the shore;
And many a lesser torrent scuds,
          With seeming roar.

Low, in a sandy valley spread,
An ancient BOROUGH rear'd her head;
Still, as in *Scottish Story* read,
          She boasts a *Race*,
To ev'ry nobler virtue bred,
          And polish'd grace.

By stately tow'r, or palace fair,
Or ruins pendent in the air,
Bold stems of Heroes, here and there,
      I could discern;
Some seem'd to muse, some seem'd to dare,
      With feature stern.

My heart did glowing transport feel,
To see a Race[1] heroic wheel,
And brandish round the deep-dy'd steel
      In sturdy blows;
While back-recoiling seem'd to reel
      Their Suthron foes.

His COUNTRY'S SAVIOUR[2], mark him well!
Bold RICHARDTON'S[3] heroic swell;
The Chief on *Sark*[4] who glorious fell,
      In high command;
And *He* whom ruthless Fates expel
      His native land.

[1] The Wallaces.
[2] William Wallace.
[3] Adam Wallace of Richardton, cousin to the immortal Preserver of Scottish Independence.
[4] Wallace Laird of Craigie, who was second in command, under Douglas Earl of Ormond, at the famous battle on the banks of Sark, fought *anno* 1448.

Spence, *parlour*; ingle-cheek, *chimney corner*; hoast, *cough*; smeek, *smoke*; rattons, *oats*; mottie, *dusty*; wauket, *horny, callonsed*; loof, *palm*; Hizzie, *wench*; eerie, *frightened*; dusht, *pushed by an ox, ram, etc*; scrimply, *barely*

To a Mouse, On turning her up in her Nest,
with the Plough, November, 1785

WEE, sleekit, cowran, tim'rous *beastie*,
O, what a panic 's in thy breastie!
Thou need na start awa sae hasty
   Wi' bickering brattle!
I wad be laith to rin an' chase thee,
   Wi' murd'ring *pattle*!

I'm truly sorry Man's dominion
Has broken Nature's social union,
An' justifies that ill opinion,
   Which makes thee startle,
At me, thy poor, earth-born companion,
   An' *fellow-mortal*!

I doubt na, whyles, but thou may *thieve*;
What then? poor beastie, thou maun live!
A *daimen-icker* in a *thrave*
   'S a sma' request:
I'll get a blessin wi' the lave,
   An' never miss 't!

Thy wee-bit *housie*, too, in ruin!
It's silly wa's the win's are strewin!
An' naething, now, to big a new ane,
   O' foggage green!
An' bleak *December's winds* ensuin,
   Baith snell an' keen!

Thou saw the fields laid bare an' wast,
An' weary *Winter* comin fast,
An' cozie here, beneath the blast,
   Thou thought to dwell,
Till crash! the cruel *coulter* past
   Out thro' thy cell.

That wee-bit heap o' leaves an' stibble,
Has cost thee monie a weary nibble!
Now thou 's turn'd out, for a' thy trouble,
      But house or hald,
To thole the Winter's *sleety dribble*,
      An' *cranreuch* cauld!

But Mousie, thou art no thy-lane,
In proving *foresight* may be vain:
The best laid schemes o' *Mice* an' *Men*,
      Gang aft agley,
An' lea'e us nought but grief an' pain,
      For promis'd joy!

Still, thou art blest, compar'd wi' *me*!
The *present* only toucheth thee:
But Och! I *backward* cast my e'e,
      On prospects drear!
An' *forward*, tho' I canna *see*,
      I *guess* an' *fear*!

sleekit, *sly, smooth*; brattle, *hurry*; pattle, *spade*; daimen-icker, *ear of corn*;
thrave, *two stooks of corn*; foggage, *rank grass*; snell, *biting*; coulter, *plough
blade*; thole, *endure*; cranreuch, *hoarfrost*; thy-lane, *alone*

The Twa Dogs. A Tale

'Twas in that place o' *Scotland's* isle,
That bears the name o' auld king COIL,
Upon a bonie day in June,
When wearing thro' the afternoon,
Twa Dogs, that were na thrang at hame,
Forgather'd ance upon a time.

The first I'll name, they ca'd him *Ceasar*,
Was keepet for his Honor's pleasure;
His hair, his size, his mouth, his lugs,
Show'd he was nane o' Scotland's dogs;
But whalpet some place far abroad,
Whare sailors gang to fish for Cod.

His locked, letter'd, braw brass-collar,
Show'd him the *gentleman* an' *scholar*;
But tho' he was o' high degree,
The fient a pride na pride had he,
But wad hae spent an hour caressan,
Ev'n wi' a Tinkler-gipsey's *messan*:
At *Kirk* or *Market*, *Mill* or *Smiddie*,
Nae tawtied *tyke*, tho' e'er sae duddie,
But he wad stan't, as glad to see him,
An' stroan't on stanes an' hillocks wi' him.

The tither was a *ploughman's collie*,
A rhyming, ranting, raving billie,
Wha for his friend an' comrade had him,
And in his freaks had *Luath* ca'd him;
After some dog in *Highlan Sang*,
Was made lang syne, lord knows how lang.

He was a gash an' faithfu' *tyke*,
As ever lap a sheugh, or dyke!
His honest sonsie, baws'nt *face*,

Ay gat him friends in ilka place;
His *breast* was white, his towzie *back*,
Weel clad wi' coat o' glossy black;
His gawsie tail, wi' upward curl,
Hung owre his hurdies wi' a swirl.

Nae doubt but they were fain o' ither,
An' unco pack an' thick the gither;
Wi' social *nose* whyles snuff'd an' snowcket;
Whyles mice an' modewurks they howcket;
Whyles scour'd awa in lang excursion,
An' worry'd ither in *diversion*;
Untill wi' daffin weary grown,
Upon a knowe they sat them down,
An' there began a lang digression
About the *lords o' the creation*.

CAESAR
I've aften wonder'd, honest *Luath*,
What sort o' life poor dogs like you have;
An' when the *gentry*'s life I saw,
What way *poor bodies* liv'd ava.

Our *Laird* gets in his racked rents,
His coals, his kane, an' a' his stents;
He rises when he likes himsel;
His flunkies answer at the bell;
He ca's his coach; he ca's his horse;
He draws a bonie, silken purse
As lang's my *tail*, whare thro' the steeks,
The yellow, letter'd *Geordie* keeks.

Frae morn to een it 's nought but toiling,
At baking, roasting, frying, boiling:
An' tho' the gentry first are steghan,
Yet ev'n the *ha' folk* fill their peghan
Wi' sauce, ragouts, an' sic like trashtrie,
That 's little short o' downright wastrie.

45

Our *Whipper-in*, wee, blastiet wonner,
Poor, worthless elf, it eats a dinner,
Better than ony *Tenant-man*
His Honor has in a' the lan':
An' what poor *Cot-folk* pit their painch in,
I own it 's past my comprehension. –

LUATH

Trowth, *Ceasar*, whyles they're fash'd eneugh;
A *Cotter* howckan in a sheugh,
Wi' dirty stanes biggan an dyke,
Bairan a quarry, an' sic like,
Himsel, a wife, he thus sustains,
A smytrie o' wee, duddie, weans,
An' nought but his han'-daurk, to keep
Them right an' tight in *thack an' raep*.

An' when they meet wi' sair disasters,
Like loss o' health, or want o' masters,
Ye maist wad think, a wee touch langer,
An' they maun starve o' cauld an' hunger:
But how it comes, I never kent yet,
They're maistly wonderfu' contented;
An' buirdly chiels, an' clever hizzies,
Are bred in sic a way as this is.

CAESAR

But then, to see how ye're negleket,
How huff'd, an' cuff'd, an' disrespeket!
L—d man, our gentry care as little
For *delvers*, *ditchers*, an' sic cattle;
They gang as saucy by poor folk,
As I wad by a stinkan brock.

I've notic'd, on our Laird's *court-day*,
An' mony a time my heart 's been wae,
Poor *tenant-bodies*, scant o' cash,
How they maun thole a *factor*'s snash;

He'll stamp an' threaten, curse an' swear,
He'll *apprehend* them, *poind* their gear,
While they maun stand, wi' aspect humble,
An' hear it a', an' fear an' tremble!

    I see how folk live that hae riches,
But surely poor-folk maun be *wretches*!

LUATH

    They're no sae wretched 's ane wad think;
Tho' constantly on poortith's brink,
They're sae accustom'd wi' the sight,
The view o't gies them little fright.

    Then chance an' fortune are sae guided,
They're ay in less or mair provided;
An' tho' fatigu'd wi' close employment,
A blink o' rest 's a sweet enjoyment.

    The dearest comfort o' their lives,
Their grushie weans, an' faithfu' wives;
The *prattling things* are just their pride,
That sweetens a' their fire-side.

    An' whyles, twalpennie-worth o' *nappy*
Can mak the bodies unco happy;
They lay aside their private cares,
To mind the Kirk an' State affairs;
They'll talk o' *patronage* an' *priests*,
Wi' kindling fury i' their breasts,
Or tell what new taxation 's comin,
An' ferlie at the folk in LON'ON.

    As bleak-fac'd Hallowmass returns,
They get the jovial, rantan *Kirns*,
When *rural life*, of ev'ry station,
Unite in common recreation;
Love blinks, Wit slaps, an' social Mirth
Forgets there 's *care* upo' the earth.

That *merry day* the year begins,
They bar the door on frosty win's;
The nappy reeks wi' mantling ream,
An' sheds a heart-inspiring steam;
The luntan pipe, an' sneeshin mill,
Are handed round wi' right guid will;
The cantie, auld folks, crackan crouse,
The young anes rantan thro' the house –
My heart has been sae fain to see them,
That I for joy hae *barket* wi' them.

Still it 's owre true that ye hae said,
Sic game is now owre aften play'd;
There 's monie a creditable *stock*
O' decent, honest, fawsont folk,
Are riven out baith root an' branch,
Some rascal's pridefu' greed to quench,
Wha thinks to knit himsel the faster
In favor wi' some *gentle Master*,
Wha, aiblins, thrang a *parliamentin*,
For *Britain's guid* his saul indentin –

CAESAR

Haith lad, ye little ken about it;
For Britain's guid! guid faith! I doubt it.
Say rather, gaun as PREMIERS lead him,
An' saying *aye* or *no* 's they bid him:
At Operas an' Plays parading,
Mortgaging, gambling, masquerading:
Or maybe, in a frolic daft,
To HAGUE or CALAIS takes a waft,
To make a *tour* an' take a whirl,
To learn *bon ton* an' see the worl'.

There, at VIENNA or VERSAILLES,
He rives his father's auld entails;
Or by MADRID he takes the rout,

To thrum *guittarres* an' fecht wi' *nowt*;
Or down *Italian Vista* startles,
Wh–re-hunting amang groves o' myrtles:
Then bowses drumlie *German-water*,
To make himsel look fair an' fatter,
An' clear the consequential sorrows,
Love-gifts of Carnival Signioras.
For Britain's guid! for her destruction!
Wi' dissipation, feud an' faction!

LUATH

Hech man! dear sirs! is that the gate,
They waste sae mony a braw estate!
Are we sae foughten an' harass'd
For gear to gang that gate at last!

O would they stay aback frae courts,
An' please themsels wi' countra sports,
It wad for ev'ry ane be better,
The *Laird*, the *Tenant*, an' the *Cotter*!
For thae frank, rantan, ramblan billies,
Fient haet o' them 's illhearted fellows;
Except for breakin o' their timmer,
Or speakin lightly o' their *Limmer*;
Or shootin of a hare or moorcock,
The ne'er-a-bit they're ill to poor folk.

But will ye tell me, master *Cesar*,
Sure *great folk*'s life 's a life o' pleasure?
Nae cauld nor hunger e'er can steer them,
The vera thought o't need na fear them.

CESAR

L—d man, were ye but whyles where I am,
The *gentles* ye wad ne'er envy them!

It's true, they needna starve or sweat,
Thro' Winter's cauld, or Summer's heat;

49

They've nae sair-wark to craze their banes,
An' fill *auld-age* wi' grips an' granes:
But *human-bodies* are sic fools,
For a' their Colledges an' Schools,
That when nae *real* ills perplex them,
They *mak* enow themsels to vex them;
An' ay the less they hae to sturt them,
In like proportion, less will hurt them.

A country fellow at the pleugh,
His *acre* 's till'd, he 's right eneugh;
A country girl at her wheel,
Her *dizzen* 's done, she 's unco weel;
But Gentlemen, an' Ladies warst,
Wi' ev'n down *want o' wark* they're curst.
They loiter, lounging, lank an' lazy;
Tho' deil-haet ails them, yet uneasy;
Their days, insipid, dull an' tasteless,
Their nights, unquiet, lang an' restless.

An' ev'n their sports, their balls an' races,
Their galloping thro' public places,
There 's sic parade, sic pomp an' art,
The joy can scarcely reach the heart.

The *Men* cast out in *party-matches*,
Then sowther a' in deep debauches.
Ae night, they're mad wi' drink an' wh–ring,
Niest day their life is past enduring.

The *Ladies* arm-in-arm in clusters,
As great an' gracious a' as sisters;
But hear their *absent thoughts* o' ither,
They're a' run-deils an' jads the gither
Whyles, owre the wee bit cup an' platie,
They sip the *scandal-potion* pretty;
Or lee-lang nights, wi' crabbet leuks,
Pore owre the devil's *pictur'd beuks*;

Stake on a chance a farmer's stackyard,
An' cheat like ony *unhang'd blackguard.*

    There 's some exceptions, man an' woman;
But this is Gentry's life in common.

    By this, the sun was out o' sight,
An' darker gloamin brought the night:
The *bum-clock* humm'd wi' lazy drone,
The kye stood rowtan i' the loan;
When up they gat, an' shook their lugs,
Rejoic'd they were na *men* but *dogs;*
An' each took off his several way,
Resolv'd to meet some ither day.

thrang, *busy;* messan, *small dog;* tyke, *dog;* duddie, *ragged;* stroan't, *pissed;*
gash, *shrewd;* sheugh, *ditch;* sonsie, *comely;* baws'nt, *brindled;* gawsie,
fine, full; hurdies, *backside;* fain o' ither, *fond of each other;* modewurk,
mole; howcket, *dug up;* kane, *fowls (paid in rent);* stents, *dues;* steeks,
stitches; Geordie, *guinea;* steghan, *filling the stomach;* peghan, *stomach;*
painch, *paunch;* bairan, *clearing;* smytrie, *collection;* thack an' raep, *thatch
and rope;* buirdly, *stalwart stout;* delvers, *labourers;* snash, *abuse;* grushie,
thriving; nappy, *ale;* ferlie, *wonder;* Hallowmass, *All Saints' Day;* Kirns,
harvest suppers; luntan, *smoking;* sneeshin mill, *snuff box;* cantie, *cheerful;*
fawsont, *respectable;* aiblins, *perhaps;* bon ton, *good breeding;* rives,
reaves; drumlie, *sedimented, cloudy;* timmer, *timber;* limmer, *mistress;*
sair-wark, *hard labour;* sowther, *patch up;* jads, *hussies;* bum-clock,
cockchafer

Scotch Drink

> *Gie him strong* Drink *until he wink,*
> *That 's sinking in despair;*
> *An'* liquor *guid, to fire his bluid,*
>   *That 's prest wi' grief an' care:*
> *There let him bowse an' deep carouse,*
>   *Wi' bumpers flowing o'er,*
> *Till he forgets his loves or debts,*
>   *An' minds his griefs no more.*
>   Solomon's Proverbs, 31: 6, 7

Let other Poets raise a fracas
'Bout vines, an' wines, an' druken *Bacchus*,
An' crabbed names an' stories wrack us,
            An' grate our lug,
I sing the juice *Scotch bear* can mak us,
            In glass or jug.

O thou, my Muse! guid, auld Scotch Drink!
Whether thro' wimplin worms thou jink,
Or, richly brown, ream owre the brink,
            In glorious faem,
Inspire me, till I *lisp* an' *wink*,
            To sing thy name!

Let husky Wheat the haughs adorn,
And Aits set up their awnie horn,
An' Pease an' Beans, at een or morn,
            Perfume the plain,
Leeze me on thee *John Barleycorn*,
            Thou king o' grain!

On thee aft Scotland chows her cood,
In souple scones, the wale o' food!
Or tumbling in the boiling flood
            Wi' kail an' beef;

52

But when thou pours thy strong *heart's blood*,
      There thou shines chief.

Food fills the wame, an' keeps us livin:
Tho' life 's a gift no worth receivin,
When heavy-dragg'd wi' pine an' grievin;
      But oil'd by thee,
The wheels o' life gae down-hill, scrievin,
      Wi' rattlin glee.

Thou clears the head o' doited Lear;
Thou chears the heart o' drooping Care;
Thou strings the nerves o' Labor-sair,
      At 's weary toil;
Thou ev'n brightens dark Despair,
      Wi' gloomy smile.

Aft, clad in massy, siller weed,
Wi' Gentles thou erects thy head;
Yet, humbly kind, in time o' need,
      The *poorman*'s wine,
His wee drap pirratch, or his bread,
      Thou kitchens fine.

Thou art the life o' public haunts;
But thee, what were our fairs an' rants?
Ev'n goodly meetings o' the saunts,
      By thee inspir'd,
When gaping they besiege the *tents*,
      Are doubly fir'd.

That *merry night* we get the corn in
O sweetly, then, thou reams the horn in!
Or reekan on a *New-year-mornin*
      In cog or bicker,
An' just a wee drap *sp'ritual burn* in,
      An' *gusty sucker*!

When Vulcan gies his bellys breath,
An' Ploughmen gather wi' their graith,
O rare! to see thee fizz an' fraeth
        I' the lugget caup!
Then *Burnewin* comes on like Death,
        At ev'ry chap.

Nae mercy, then, for airn *or* steel;
The brawnie, banie, Ploughman-chiel
Brings hard owrehip, wi' sturdy wheel,
        The strong forehammer,
Till block an' studdie ring an' reel
        Wi' dinsome clamour.

When skirlin weanies see the light,
Thou maks the gossips clatter bright,
How fumbling coofs their dearies slight,
        Wae worth the name!
Nae Howdie gets a social night,
        Or plack frae them.

When neebors anger at a plea,
An' just as wud as wud can be,
How easy can the *barley-bree*
        Cement the quarrel!
It 's ay the cheapest Lawyer's fee
        To taste the barrel.

Alake! that e'er my *Muse* has reason
To wyte her countrymen wi' treason!
But mony daily weet their weason
        Wi' liquors nice,
An' hardly, in a winter season,
        E'er spier her price.

Wae worth that *Brandy*, burnan trash!
Fell source o' monie a pain an' brash!
Twins mony a poor, doylt, druken hash
   O' half his days;
An' sends, beside, auld *Scotland*'s cash
   To her warst faes.

Ye Scots wha wish auld Scotland well,
Ye chief, to you my tale I tell,
Poor, plackless devils like *mysel*,
   It sets you ill,
Wi' bitter, dearthfu' *wines* to mell,
   Or *foreign gill*.

May *Gravels* round his blather wrench,
An' *Gouts* torment him, inch by inch,
Wha twists his gruntle wi' a glunch
   O' sour disdain,
Out owre a glass o' *Whisky-punch*
   Wi' honest men!

O *Whisky*! soul o' plays an' pranks!
Accept a *Bardie*'s gratefu' thanks!
When wanting thee, what tuneless cranks
   Are my poor Verses!
Thou comes – they rattle i' their ranks
   At ither's arses!

Thee, *Ferintosh*! O sadly lost!
Scotland lament frae coast to coast!
Now colic-grips, an' barkin hoast,
   May kill us a';
For loyal *Forbes' Charter'd boast*
   Is taen awa!

Thae curst horse-leeches o' th' Excise,
Wha mak the *Whisky stills* their prize!
Haud up thy han' *Deil*! ance, twice, thrice!
      There, sieze the blinkers!
An' bake them up in brunstane pies
        For poor damn'd *Drinkers*.

Fortune, if thou'll but gie me still
Hale breeks, a scone, an' *Whisky gill*,
An' rowth o' *rhyme* to rave at will,
      Tak a' the rest,
An' deal 't about as thy blind skill
        Directs thee best.

wimplin, *twisting*; worms, *spiral tubes on a still*; aits, *oats*; wale, *best*;
scrievin, *to glide along*; cog, *wooden drinking vessel*; bicker, *drinking vessel
with handle*; Burnewin, *blacksmith*; studdie, *anvil*; gossips, *godmothers
(women friends present at a birth)*; howdie, *midwife*; wud, *enraged*;
weason, *gullet*; spier, *ask*; blather, *bladder*; glunch, *scowl*; rowth,
abundance

Brose and Butter

JENNY sits up i' the laft,
    Jockie wad fain a been at her;
But there cam a wind out o' the west
    Made a' the winnocks to clatter.

    O gie my love brose, lasses;
        O gie my love brose and butter;
    For nane in Carrick wi' him
        Can gie a c—t its supper.

The laverock lo'es the grass,
    The paetrick lo'es the stibble:
And hey, for the gardiner lad,
    To gully awa wi' his dibble!
      O gie, &c.

My daddie sent me to the hill
    To pu' my minnie some heather;
An' drive it in your fill,
    Ye're welcome to the leather.
      O gie, &c.

The Mouse is a merry wee beast,
    The Moudiewart wants the een;
And O, for a touch o' the thing
    I had in my nieve yestreen.
      O gie, &c.

We a' were fou yestreen,
    The night shall be its brither;
And hey, for a roaring pin
    To nail twa wames thegither!
      O gie, &c.

winnocks, *windows*; brose, *porridge*; laverock, *lark*; minnie, *mother*;
moudiewart, *mole*; nieve, *fist*; pin, *skewer*; wame, *belly*

Sketch

HAIL, Poesie! thou nymph reserv'd!
In chase o' thee, what crowds hae swerv'd
Frae Common Sense, or sunk ennerv'd
    'Mang heaps o' clavers;
And Och! o'er aft thy joes hae starv'd
    'Mid a' thy favors!

Say, Lassie, why thy train amang,
While loud the trumps heroic clang,
And Sock and buskin skelp alang
    To death or marriage;
Scarce ane has tried the Shepherd-sang
    But wi' miscarriage?

In Homer's craft Jock Milton thrives;
Eschylus' pen Will Shakespeare drives;
Wee Pope, the knurlin, 'till him rives
    Horatian fame;
In thy sweet sang, Barbauld, survives
    E'en Sappho's flame.

But thee, Theocritus, wha matches?
They're no' Herd's ballats, Maro's catches;
Squire Pope but busks his skinklin patches
    O' Heathen tatters:
I pass by hunders, nameless wretches,
    That ape their betters.

In this braw age o' wit and lear,
Will nane the Shepherd's whistle mair
Blaw sweetly in his native air
    And rural grace;
And wi' the far-fam'd Grecian share
    A rival place?

Yes! there is ane: a Scotish callan!
There 's ane: come forrit, honest Allan!
Thou need na jouk behint the hallan,
    A chiel sae clever;
The teeth o' Time may gnaw Tamtallan,
    But thou 's for ever.

Thou paints auld Nature to the nines,
In thy sweet Caledonian lines;
Nae gowden stream thro' myrtles twines
    Where Philomel,
While nightly breezes sweep the vines,
    Her griefs will tell!

Thy rural loves are Nature's sel';
Nae bombast spates o' nonsense swell;
Nae snap conceits, but that sweet spell
    O' witchin' loove,
That charm that can the strongest quell,
    The sternest move.

In gowany glens thy burnie strays,
where bonie lasses bleach their claes;
Or trots by hazelly shaws and braes
    Wi' hawthorns gray,
Where blackbirds join the shepherd's lays
    At close o' day.

clavers, *idle talk*; joes, *sweethearts*; knurlin, *dwarf*; skinklin, *showy, glittering*; callan, *boy*; hallan, *partition wall*; claes, *clothes*

To a Louse, On Seeing one on
a Lady's Bonnet at Church

HA! whare ye gaun, ye crowlan ferlie!
Your impudence protects you sairly:
I canna say but ye strunt rarely,
   Owre *gawze* and *lace*;
Tho' faith, I fear ye dine but sparely,
   On sic a place.

Ye ugly, creepan, blastet wonner,
Detested, shunn'd, by saunt an' sinner,
How daur ye set your fit upon her,
   Sae fine a *Lady*!
Gae somewhere else and seek your dinner,
   On some poor body.

Swith, in some beggar's haffet squattle;
There ye may creep, and sprawl, and sprattle,
Wi' ither kindred, jumping cattle,
   In shoals and nations;
Whare *horn* nor *bane* ne'er daur unsettle,
   Your thick plantations.

Now haud you there, ye're out o' sight,
Below the fatt'rels, snug and tight,
Na faith ye yet! ye'll no be right,
   Till ye've got on it,
The vera tapmost, towrin height
   O' *Miss's bonnet*.

My sooth! right bauld ye set your nose out,
As plump an' gray as onie grozet:
O for some rank, mercurial rozet,
   Or fell, red smeddum,
I'd gie you sic a hearty dose o't,
   Wad dress your droddum!

I wad na been surpriz'd to spy
You on an auld wife's *flainen toy*;
Or aiblins some bit duddie boy,
      On 's *wylecoat*;
But Miss's fine *Lunardi*, fye!
        How daur ye do 't?

O *Jenny* dinna toss your head,
An' set your beauties a' abread!
Ye little ken what cursed speed
      The blastie 's makin!
Thae *winks* and *finger-ends*, I dread,
      Are notice takin!

O wad some Pow'r the giftie gie us
To see oursels as others see us!
It wad frae monie a blunder free us
      An' foolish notion:
What airs in dress an' gait wad lea'e us,
      And ev'n Devotion!

strunt, *move with assurance*; haffet, *temple*, fatt'rels, *ribbon ends*; grozet,
gooseberry; rozet, *resin*; smeddum, *insecticide powder*; dress your
droddum, *thrash your backside*; flainen, *flannel*; toy, *cap*; wylecoat,
flannel vest; Lunardi, *kind of bonnet*; blastie, *ill-tempered beast*

To a Mountain-Daisy, On turning one down,
with the Plough, in April – 1786

Wee, modest, crimson-tipped flow'r,
Thou 's met me in an evil hour;
For I maun crush amang the stoure
         Thy slender stem:
To spare thee now is past my pow'r,
         Thou bonie gem.

Alas! it 's no thy neebor sweet,
The bonie *Lark*, companion meet!
Bending thee 'mang the dewy weet!
         Wi 's spreckl'd breast,
When upward-springing, blythe, to greet
         The purpling East.

Cauld blew the bitter-biting *North*
Upon thy early, humble birth;
Yet chearfully thou glinted forth
         Amid the storm,
Scarce rear'd above the *Parent-earth*
         Thy tender form.

The flaunting *flow'rs* our Gardens yield,
High-shelt'ring woods and wa's maun shield,
But thou, beneath the random bield
         O' clod or stane,
Adorns the histie *stibble-field*,
         Unseen, alane.

There, in thy scanty mantle clad,
Thy snawie bosom sun-ward spread,
Thou lifts thy unassuming head
         In humble guise;
But now the *share* uptears thy bed,
         And low thou lies!

Such is the fate of artless Maid,
Sweet *flow'ret* of the rural shade!
By Love's simplicity betray'd,
      And guileless trust,
Till she, like thee, all soil'd, is laid
      Low i' the dust.

Such is the fate of simple Bard,
On Life's rough ocean luckless starr'd!
Unskilful he to note the card
      Of *prudent Lore*,
Till billows rage, and gales blow hard,
      And whelm him o'er!

Such fate to *suffering worth* is giv'n,
Who long with wants and woes has striv'n,
By human pride or cunning driv'n
      To Mis'ry's brink,
Till wrench'd of ev'ry stay but HEAV'N,
      He, ruin'd, sink!

Ev'n thou who mourn'st the *Daisy*'s fate,
That fate is thine – no distant date;
Stern Ruin's *plough-share* drives, elate,
      Full on thy bloom,
Till crush'd beneath the *furrow*'s weight,
      Shall be thy doom!

stoure, *dust*; bield, *shelter*; histie, *dry*, *stony*

Epitaph on a Wag in Mauchline

Lament 'im Mauchline husbands a',
    He aften did assist ye;
For had ye staid whole weeks awa'
    Your wives they ne'er had miss'd ye.

Ye Mauchline bairns as on ye pass,
    To school in bands thegither,
O tread ye lightly on his grass,
    Perhaps he was your father.

The Northern Lass

Though cruel Fate should bid us part,
　　Far as the Pole and Line,
Her dear idea round my heart
　　Should tenderly entwine:

Though mountains rise, and desarts howl,
　　And oceans roar between;
Yet dearer than my deathless soul
　　I still would love my Jean.

To a Haggis

Fair fa' your honest, sonsie face,
Great Chieftan o' the Puddin-race!
Aboon them a' ye tak your place,
        Painch, tripe, or thairm:
Weel are ye wordy of a *grace*
        As lang 's my arm.

The groaning trencher there ye fill,
Your hurdies like a distant hill,
Your *pin* wad help to mend a mill
        In time o' need,
While thro' your pores the dews distil
        Like amber bead.

His knife see Rustic-labour dight,
An' cut you up wi' ready slight,
Trenching your gushing entrails bright
        Like onie ditch;
And then, O what a glorious sight,
        Warm-reekin, rich!

Then, horn for horn they stretch an' strive,
Deil tak the hindmost, on they drive,
Till a' their weel-swall'd kytes belyve
        Are bent like drums;
Then auld Guidman, maist like to rive,
        Bethankit hums.

Is there that owre his French *ragout*,
Or *olio* that wad staw a sow,
Or *fricassee* wad mak her spew
        Wi' perfect sconner,
Looks down wi' sneering, scornfu' view
        On sic a dinner?

Poor devil! see him owre his trash,
As feckless as a wither'd rash,
His spindle shank a guid whip-lash,
 His nieve a nit;
Thro' bluidy flood or field to dash,
 O how unfit!

But mark the Rustic, *haggis-fed*,
The trembling earth resounds his tread,
Clap in his walie nieve a blade,
 He'll mak it whissle;
An' legs, an' arms, an' heads will sned,
 Like taps o' thrissle.

Ye Pow'rs wha mak mankind your care,
And dish them out their bill o' fare,
Auld Scotland wants nae skinking ware
 That jaups in luggies;
But, if ye wish her gratefu' pray'r,
 Gie her a *Haggis*!

thairm, *intestines*; pin, *skewer*; kytes, *bellies*; belyve, *soon*; Bethankit, *grace after meal*; olio, *heavily spiced stew*; staw, *fill up*; sconner, *disgust*; nit, *nut*; walie, *large, ample*; jaups, *jerks*; luggies, *wooden dish*

To Miss Ferrier

MADAM
    NAE Heathen Name shall I prefix,
        Frae Pindus or Parnassus;
    AULD REEKIE dings them a' to sticks
        For rhyme-inspiring Lasses. –

Jove's tunefu' Dochters three times three
    Made Homer deep their debtor;
But gien the body half an e'e,
    Nine FERRIERS wad done better. –

Last day my mind was in a bog,
    Down George's street I stoited;
A creeping, cauld PROSAIC fog
    My vera senses doited. –

Do what I dought to set her free,
    My Muse lay in the mire;
Ye turn'd a neuk – I saw your e'e –
    She took the wing like fire. –

The mournfu' Sang I here inclose,
    In GRATITUDE I send you;
And pray in rhyme, sincere as prose,
    A' GUDE THINGS MAY ATTEND YOU.

                       ROB^t. BURNS

St James' Square⎱
Saturday even: ⎰

stoited, *staggered*; doited, *muddled*; neuk, *corner*

Ca' the Ewes

Cᴀ' the ewes to the knowes,
Ca' them whare the heather grows,
Ca' them whare the burnie rowes,
  My bonie Dearie. –

As I gaed down the water-side
There I met my Shepherd-lad,
He row'd me sweetly in his plaid,
  And he ca'd me his Dearie. –
    Ca' the &c.

Will ye gang down the water-side
And see the waves sae sweetly glide
Beneath the hazels spreading wide,
  The moon it shines fu' clearly. –
    Ca' the &c.

I was bred up at nae sic school,
My Shepherd-lad, to play the fool;
And a' the day to sit in dool,
  And naebody to see me. –
    Ca' the &c.

Ye sall get gowns and ribbons meet,
Cauf-leather shoon upon your feet,
And in my arms ye 'se lie and sleep,
  And ye sall be my Dearie. –
    Ca' the &c.

If ye'll but stand to what ye've said,
I 'se gang wi' you, my Shepherd-lad,
And ye may rowe me in your plaid,
  And I sall be your Dearie. –
    Ca' the &c.

While waters wimple to the sea;
While Day blinks in the lift sae hie;
Till clay-cauld Death sall blin' my e'e,
    Ye sall be my Dearie. –
        Ca' the ewes &c.

rowes, *rolls*; dool, *sorrow*

Whistle o'er the Lave o't

FIRST when Maggy was my care,
Heaven, I thought, was in her air;
Now we're married – spier nae mair –
  Whistle o'er the lave o't. –

Meg was meek, and Meg was mild,
Sweet and harmless as a child –
Wiser men than me 's beguil'd;
  Whistle o'er the lave o't. –

How we live, my Meg and me,
How we love and how we gree;
I carena by how few may see,
  Whistle o'er the lave o't. –

Wha I wish were maggots' meat,
Dish'd up in her winding-sheet;
I could write – but Meg maun see 't –
  Whistle o'er the lave o't. –

spier, *ask*; gree, *agree*

To Mr John Taylor

With Pegasus upon a day
   Apollo, weary flying,
(Thro' frosty hills the journey lay)
   On foot the way was plying. –

Poor, slip-shod, giddy Pegasus
   Was but a sorry walker,
To Vulcan then Apollo gaes
   To get a frosty calker. –

Oblidging Vulcan fell to wark,
   Threw by his coat and bonnet;
And did Sol's business in a crack,
   Sol pay'd him with a sonnet. –

Ye Vulcan's Sons of Wanlockhead,
   Pity my sad disaster,
My Pegasus is poorly shod,
   I'll pay you like my Master. –

The Cares o' Love

HE
THE cares o' Love are sweeter far
  Than onie other pleasure;
And if sae dear its sorrows are
  Enjoyment, what a treasure!

SHE
I fear to try, I dare na try
  A passion sae ensnaring;
For light 's her heart and blythe 's her song
  That for nae man is caring.

Louis what Reck I by Thee

Louis, what reck I by thee,
  Or Geordie on his ocean:
Dyvor, beggar louns to me,
  I reign in Jeanie's bosom.

Let her crown my love her law,
  And in her breast enthrone me:
Kings and nations, swith awa!
  Reif randies I disown ye! –

reck, *heed*; dyvor, *bankrupt*; louns, *fellows*; reif, *thieving*; randies, *roughs*

Robin Shure in Hairst

Robin shure in hairst,
   I shure wi' him;
Fint a heuk had I,
   Yet I stack by him.

I gaed up to Dunse,
   To warp a wab o' plaiden;
At his daddie's yet,
   Wha met me but Robin.
     Robin shure &c.

Was na Robin bauld,
   Tho' I was a cotter,
Play'd me sic a trick
   And me the Eller's dochter!
     Robin shure &c.

Robin promis'd me
   A' my winter vittle;
Fient haet he had but three
   Goos feathers and a whittle.
     Robin shure &c.

shure, *reap with a sickle*; hairst, *harvest*; heuk, *sickle*; warp, *weave*; cotter, *cottager*; eller, *elder*; whittle, *knife*

Come Rede Me, Dame

I

'COME rede me, dame, come tell me, dame,
   'My dame come tell me truly,
'What length o' graith, when weel ca'd hame,
   'Will sair a woman duly?'
The carlin clew her wanton tail,
   Her wanton tail sae ready –
I learn'd a sang in Annandale,
   Nine inch will please a lady. –

II

But for a koontrie c–nt like mine,
   In sooth, we're nae sae gentle;
We'll tak tway thumb-bread to the nine,
   And that 's a sonsy p–ntle:
O Leeze me on my Charlie lad,
   I'll ne'er forget my Charlie!
Tway roarin handfu's and a daud,
   He nidge't it in fu' rarely. –

III

But weary fa' the laithron doup,
   And may it ne'er be thrivin!
It 's no the length that maks me loup,
   But it 's the double drivin. –
Come nidge me, Tam, come nudge me, Tam,
   Come nidge me o'er the nyvel!
Come lowse and lug your battering ram,
   And thrash him at my gyvel!

rede, *tell, advise*; graith, *gear, penis*; sair, *serve*; carlin, *old woman, witch*;
clew, *scratched*; thumb-bread, *thumb's breadth*; laithron, *lazy*; doup,
backside; loup, *jump*; gyvel, *gable*

Lassie Lie Near Me

Lang hae we parted been,
   Lassie my dearie;
Now we are met again,
   Lassie lie near me.
     Near me, near me,
     Lassie lie near me;
     Lang hast thou lien thy lane,
     Lassie lie near me.

A' that I hae endur'd,
   Lassie, my dearie,
Here in thy arms is cur'd,
   Lassie lie near me.
     Near me, &c.

John Anderson My Joe

John Anderson my jo, John,
    When we were first acquent;
Your locks were like the raven,
    Your bony brow was brent;
But now your brow is beld, John,
    Your locks are like the snaw;
But blessings on your frosty pow,
    John Anderson my Jo.

John Anderson my jo, John,
    We clamb the hill the gither;
And mony a canty day, John,
    We've had wi' ane anither:
Now we maun totter down, John,
    And hand in hand we'll go;
And sleep the gither at the foot,
    John Anderson my Jo.

Tam o' Shanter. A Tale

Of Brownyis and of Bogillis full is this buke.

Gawin Douglas.

WHEN chapman billies leave the street,
And drouthy neebors, neebors meet,
As market-days are wearing late,
An' folk begin to tak the gate;
While we sit bousing at the nappy,
And getting fou and unco happy,
We think na on the lang Scots miles,
The mosses, waters, slaps, and styles,
That lie between us and our hame,
Whare sits our sulky sullen dame,
Gathering her brows like gathering storm,
Nursing her wrath to keep it warm.

This truth fand honest *Tam o' Shanter*,
As he frae Ayr ae night did canter,
(Auld Ayr, wham ne'er a town surpasses,
For honest men and bonny lasses.)

O *Tam*! hadst thou but been sae wise,
As ta'en thy ain wife *Kate*'s advice!
She tauld thee weel thou was a skellum,
A blethering, blustering, drunken blellum;
That frae November till October,
Ae market-day thou was nae sober;
That ilka melder, wi' the miller,
Thou sat as lang as thou had siller;
That every naig was ca'd a shoe on,
The smith and thee gat roaring fou on;
That at the L—d 's house, even on Sunday,
Thou drank wi' Kirkton Jean till Monday.
She prophesied that late or soon,
Thou would be found deep drown'd in Doon;

Or catch'd wi' warlocks in the mirk,
By *Alloway*'s auld haunted kirk.

Ah, gentle dames! it gars me greet,
To think how mony counsels sweet,
How mony lengthen'd sage advices,
The husband frae the wife despises!

But to our tale: Ae market-night,
Tam had got planted unco right;
Fast by an ingle, bleezing finely,
Wi' reaming swats, that drank divinely;
And at his elbow, Souter *Johnny*,
His ancient, trusty, drouthy crony;
Tam lo'ed him like a vera brither;
They had been fou for weeks thegither.
The night drave on wi' sangs and clatter;
And ay the ale was growing better:
The landlady and *Tam* grew gracious,
Wi' favours, secret, sweet, and precious:
The Souter tauld his queerest stories;
The landlord's laugh was ready chorus:
The storm without might rair and rustle,
Tam did na mind the storm a whistle.

Care, mad to see a man sae happy,
E'en drown'd himsel amang the nappy:
As bees flee hame wi' lades o' treasure,
The minutes wing'd their way wi' pleasure:
Kings may be blest, but *Tam* was glorious,
O'er a' the ills o' life victorious!

But pleasures are like poppies spread,
You seize the flower, its bloom is shed;
Or like the snow falls in the river,
A moment white – then melts for ever;
Or like the borealis race,
That flit ere you can point their place;

Or like the rainbow's lovely form
Evanishing amid the storm. –
Nae man can tether time or tide;
The hour approaches *Tam* maun ride;
That hour, o' night's black arch the key-stane,
That dreary hour he mounts his beast in;
And sic a night he taks the road in,
As ne'er poor sinner was abroad in.

The wind blew as 'twad blawn its last;
The rattling showers rose on the blast;
The speedy gleams the darkness swallow'd;
Loud, deep, and lang, the thunder bellow'd:
That night, a child might understand,
The Deil had business on his hand.

Weel mounted on his gray mare, *Meg*,
A better never lifted leg,
Tam skelpit on thro' dub and mire,
Despising wind, and rain, and fire;
Whiles holding fast his gude blue bonnet;
Whiles crooning o'er some auld Scots sonnet;
Whiles glowring round wi' prudent cares,
Lest bogles catch him unawares:
Kirk-Alloway was drawing nigh,
Whare ghaists and houlets nightly cry. –

By this time he was cross the ford,
Whare, in the snaw, the chapman smoor'd;
And past the birks and meikle stane,
Whare drunken *Charlie* brak 's neck-bane;
And thro' the whins, and by the cairn,
Whare hunters fand the murder'd bairn;
And near the thorn, aboon the well,
Whare *Mungo*'s mither hang'd hersel. –
Before him *Doon* pours all his floods;
The doubling storm roars thro' the woods;

The lightnings flash from pole to pole;
Near and more near the thunders roll:
When, glimmering thro' the groaning trees,
Kirk-Alloway seem'd in a bleeze;
Thro' ilka bore the beams were glancing;
And loud resounded mirth and dancing. –

Inspiring bold *John Barleycorn*!
What dangers thou canst make us scorn!
Wi' tippeny, we fear nae evil;
Wi' usquabae, we'll face the devil! –
The swats sae ream'd in *Tammie*'s noddle,
Fair play, he car'd na deils a boddle.
But *Maggie* stood right sair astonish'd,
Till, by the heel and hand admonish'd,
She ventured forward on the light;
And, vow! *Tam* saw an unco sight!
Warlocks and witches in a dance;
Nae cotillion brent new frae *France*,
But hornpipes, jigs, strathspeys, and reels,
Put life and mettle in their heels.
A winnock-bunker in the east,
There sat auld Nick, in shape o' beast;
A towzie tyke, black, grim, and large,
To gie them music was his charge:
He screw'd the pipes and gart them skirl,
Till roof and rafters a' did dirl. –
Coffins stood round, like open presses,
That shaw'd the dead in their last dresses;
And by some devilish cantraip slight
Each in its cauld hand held a light. –
By which heroic *Tam* was able
To note upon the haly table,
A murderer's banes in gibbet airns;
Twa span-lang, wee, unchristen'd bairns;
A thief, new-cutted frae a rape,

Wi' his last gasp his gab did gape;
Five tomahawks, wi' blude red-rusted;
Five scymitars, wi' murder crusted;
A garter, which a babe had strangled;
A knife, a father's throat had mangled,
Whom his ain son o' life bereft,
The grey hairs yet stack to the heft;
Wi' mair o' horrible and awefu',
Which even to name wad be unlawfu'.

As *Tammie* glow'rd, amaz'd, and curious,
The mirth and fun grew fast and furious:
The piper loud and louder blew;
The dancers quick and quicker flew;
They reel'd, they set, they cross'd, they cleekit,
Till ilka carlin swat and reekit,
And coost her duddies to the wark,
And linket at it in her sark!

Now, *Tam*, O *Tam*! had thae been queans,
A' plump and strapping in their teens,
Their sarks, instead o' creeshie flannen,
Been snaw-white seventeen hunder linnen!
Thir breeks o' mine, my only pair,
That ance were plush, o' gude blue hair,
I wad hae gi'en them off my hurdies,
For ae blink o' the bonie burdies!

But wither'd beldams, auld and droll,
Rigwoodie hags wad spean a foal,
Lowping and flinging on a crummock,
I wonder didna turn thy stomach.

But *Tam* kend what was what fu' brawlie,
There was ae winsome wench and wawlie,
That night enlisted in the core,
(Lang after kend on *Carrick* shore;
For mony a beast to dead she shot,

And perish'd mony a bony boat,
And shook baith meikle corn and bear,
And kept the country-side in fear:)
Her cutty sark, o' Paisley harn,
That while a lassie she had worn,
In longitude tho' sorely scanty,
It was her best, and she was vauntie. –
Ah! little kend thy reverend grannie,
That sark she coft for her wee Nannie,
Wi' twa pund Scots, ('twas a' her riches),
Wad ever grac'd a dance of witches!

But here my Muse her wing maun cour;
Sic flights are far beyond her pow'r;
To sing how Nannie lap and flang,
(A souple jade she was, and strang),
And how *Tam* stood, like ane bewitch'd,
And thought his very een enrich'd;
Even Satan glowr'd, and fidg'd fu' fain,
And hotch'd and blew wi' might and main:
Till first ae caper, syne anither,
Tam tint his reason a' thegither,
And roars out, 'Weel done, Cutty-sark!'
And in an instant all was dark:
And scarcely had he Maggie rallied,
When out the hellish legion sallied.

As bees bizz out wi' angry fyke,
When plundering herds assail their byke;
As open pussie's mortal foes,
When, pop! she starts before their nose;
As eager runs the market-crowd,
When 'Catch the thief!' resounds aloud;
So Maggie runs, the witches follow,
Wi' mony an eldritch skreech and hollow.

Ah, *Tam*! Ah, *Tam*! thou'll get thy fairin!
In hell they'll roast thee like a herrin!
In vain thy *Kate* awaits thy comin!
Kate soon will be a woefu' woman!
Now, do thy speedy utmost, Meg,
And win the key-stane of the brig;
There at them thou thy tail may toss,
A running stream they dare na cross.
But ere the key-stane she could make,
The fient a tail she had to shake!
For Nannie, far before the rest,
Hard upon noble Maggie prest,
And flew at *Tam* wi' furious ettle;
But little wist she Maggie's mettle –
Ae spring brought off her master hale,
But left behind her ain gray tail:
The carlin claught her by the rump,
And left poor Maggie scarce a stump.

Now, wha this tale o' truth shall read,
Ilk man and mother's son, take heed:
Whene'er to drink you are inclin'd,
Or cutty-sarks run in your mind,
Think, ye may buy the joys o'er dear,
Remember Tam o' Shanter's mare.

chapman billies, *pedlar fellows*; drouthy, *thirsty*; nappy, *ale*; skellum, *scoundrel*; blellum, *idle babbler*; melder, *the occasion of grinding a customer's corn at the mill*; swats, *ale*; souter, *cobbler*; skelpit, *sped*; bogle, *ghost, goblin*; houlet, *owl*; smoor'd, *smothered*; birk, *birch*; meikle, *big*; usquabae, *whisky*; winnock-bunker, *seat by a window*; cantraip, *magic*; airns, *irons*; cleekit, *linked arms*; swat, *sweated*; duddies, *rags*; wark, *work*; linket, *skipped*; sark, *shirt*; creeshie, *greasy, filthy*; rigwoodie, *withered*; spean, *wean*; crummock, *crook*; wawlie, *fine, ample*; harn, *coarse linen*; vauntie, *vain, proud*; coft, *bought*; cour, *fold*; fyke, *commotion*

Song

Ae fond kiss, and then we sever;
Ae farewell, and then for ever!
Deep in heart-wrung tears I'll pledge thee,
Warring sighs and groans I'll wage thee. –

Who shall say that Fortune grieves him,
While the star of hope she leaves him:
Me, nae chearful twinkle lights me;
Dark despair around benights me. –

 I'll ne'er blame my partial fancy,
Naething could resist my Nancy:
But to see her, was to love her;
Love but her, and love for ever. –

Had we never lov'd sae kindly,
Had we never lov'd sae blindly!
Never met – or never parted,
We had ne'er been broken-hearted. –

Fare-thee-weel, thou first and fairest!
Fare-thee-weel, thou best and dearest!
Thine be ilka joy and treasure,
Peace, Enjoyment, Love and Pleasure! –

Ae fond kiss, and then we sever!
Ae fareweel, Alas, for ever!
Deep in heart-wrung tears I'll pledge thee,
Warring sighs and groans I'll wage thee. –

Open the Door to Me Oh

Oh, open the door, some pity to shew,
    If love it may na be, Oh;
Tho' thou hast been false, I'll ever prove true,
    Oh, open the door to me, Oh.

Cauld is the blast upon my pale cheek,
    But caulder thy love for me, Oh:
The frost that freezes the life at my heart,
    Is nought to my pains frae thee, Oh.

The wan moon sets behind the white wave,
    And time is setting with me, Oh:
False friends, false love, farewell! for mair
    I'll ne'er trouble them, nor thee, Oh.

She has open'd the door, she has open'd it wide,
    She sees his pale corse on the plain, Oh:
My true love! she cried, and sank down by his side,
    Never to rise again, Oh.

Address to the Tooth-Ache

My curse on your envenom'd stang,
That shoots my tortur'd gums alang,
An' thro' my lugs gies mony a bang
        Wi' gnawin vengeance;
Tearing my nerves wi' bitter twang,
        Like racking engines.

A' down my beard the slavers trickle,
I cast the wee stools owre the meikle,
While round the fire the hav'rels keckle,
        To see me loup;
I curse an' ban, an' wish a heckle
        Were i' their doup.

Whan fevers burn, or agues freeze us,
Rheumatics gnaw, or colics squeeze us,
Our neebors sympathize, to ease us,
        Wi' pitying moan;
But thou – the hell o' a' diseases,
        They mock our groan.

O' a' the num'rous human dools,
Ill har'sts, daft bargains, *cutty-stools*,
Or worthy friends laid i' the mools,
        Sad sight to see!
The tricks o' knaves, or fash o' fools,
        Thou bear'st the gree.

Whare'er that place be, priests ca' hell,
Whare a' the tones o' mis'ry yell,
An' plagues in ranked number tell
        In deadly raw,
Thou, *Tooth-ache*, surely bear'st the bell
        Aboon them a'!

O! thou grim mischief-makin chiel,
That gars the notes o' discord squeel,
Till human-kind aft dance a reel
   In gore a shoe thick,
Gie a' the faes o' Scotland's weal
   A Towmond's Tooth-Ache!

hav'rel, *halfwit*; heckle, *flax comb*; cutty-stool, *stool of repentance in church*; mools, *grave-clods*; gree, *supremacy*

Oh Wert Thou in the Cauld Blast

Oʜ wert thou in the cauld blast,
　　On yonder lea, on yonder lea;
My plaidie to the angry airt,
　　I'd shelter thee, I'd shelter thee:
Or did misfortune's bitter storms
　　Around thee blaw, around thee blaw,
Thy bield should be my bosom,
　　To share it a', to share it a'.

Or were I in the wildest waste,
　　Sae black and bare, sae black and bare,
The desart were a paradise,
　　If thou wert there, if thou wert there.
Or were I monarch o' the globe,
　　Wi' thee to reign, wi' thee to reign;
The brightest jewel in my crown,
　　Wad be my queen, wad be my queen.

airt, *direction*; bield, *shelter*

Burns Grace at Kirkudbright

Some have meat and cannot eat,
    Some can not eat that want it:
But we have meat and we can eat,
    Sae let the Lord be thankit.

Epitaph on D— C—

HERE lies in earth a root of H–ll,
  .Set by the Deil's ain dibble;
This worthless body d—d himsel,
  To save the L—d the trouble.

Had I the Wyte she Bade Me

Had I the wyte, had I the wyte,
  Had I the wyte, she bade me;
She watch'd me by the hie-gate-side,
  And up the loan she shaw'd me;
And when I wad na venture in,
  A coward loon she ca'd me:
Had Kirk and State been in the gate,
  I lighted when she bade me. –

Sae craftilie she took me ben,
  And bade me mak nae clatter;
'For our ramgunshoch, glum Goodman
  'Is o'er ayont the water:'
Whae'er shall say I wanted grace,
  When I did kiss and dawte her,
Let him be planted in my place,
  Syne, say, I was a fautor. –

Could I for shame, could I for shame,
  Could I for shame refus'd her;
And wad na Manhood been to blame,
  Had I unkindly us'd her:
He claw'd her wi' the ripplin-kame,
  And blae and bluidy bruis'd her;
When sic a husband was frae hame,
  What wife but wad excus'd her?

I dighted ay her een sae blue,
   And bann'd the cruel randy;
And weel I wat her willin mou
   Was e'en like succarcandie.
At glomin-shote it was, I wat,
   I lighted on the Monday;
But I cam thro' the Tiseday's dew
   To wanton Willie's brandy.

ramgunshoch, *ill-tempered*; dawte, *caress*; fautor, *defaulter, wrong-doer*; ripplin-kame, *flax comb*; dighted, *dried*; mou, *mouth*; wat, *knew*; glomin-shote, *twilight interval before using lights indoors*

94

The Trogger

As I cam down by Annan side,
   Intending for the border,
Amang the Scroggie banks and braes,
   Wha met I but a trogger.
He laid me down upon my back,
   I thought he was but jokin,
Till he was in me to the hilts,
   O the deevil tak sic troggin!

What could I say, what could I do,
   I bann'd and sair misca'd him,
But whiltie-whaltie gae'd his a—e
   The mair that I forbade him:
He stell'd his foot against a stane,
   And doubl'd ilka stroke in,
Till I gaed daft amang his hands,
   O the deevil tak sic troggin!

Then up we raise, and took the road,
   And in by Ecclefechan,
Where the brandy-stoup we gart it clink,
   And the strang-beer ream the quech in.
Bedown the bents o' Bonshaw braes,
   We took the partin' yokin';
But I've claw'd a sairy c—t synsine,
   O the deevil tak sic troggin!

trogger, *trucker, pedlar*; gart, *made*; ream, *froth*; quech, *quaich, drinking vessel*; bents, *hillsides*

Bonnie Peg

As I cam in by our gate-end,
    As day was waxen weary,
O wha cam tripping down the street
    But bonnie Peg, my dearie!

Her air sae sweet, and shape complete,
    Wi' nae proportion wanting,
The queen of love did never move
    Wi' motion mair enchanting.

Wi' linked hands we took the sands
    Adown yon winding river;
And, oh! that hour, and broomy bower,
    Can I forget it ever!